READWELL'S

LEARN [MARATHI]
IN A [MONTH]

Easy Method of Learning Marathi
Through English Without a Teacher

MEDHA VELANKAR
M.A.

Readwell Publications
NEW DELHI-110008

Published by:
READWELL PUBLICATIONS
B-8, Rattan Jyoti, 18, Rajendra Place
New Delhi-110 008 (INDIA)
Phone : 25737448, 25721761, 25712649
Fax : 91-11-25812385
E-mail : readwell@sify.com
        newlight@vsnl.net

ISBN 81-87782-02-1

Printed at : Arya Offset Press, New Delhi.

PREFACE

At a time when there is being felt greater and greater need for learning more and more regional languages, this book on Marathi will come as a boon. For people who know Hindi or Sanskrit, the Marathi language is easy to learn, yet we have tried to teach this through English because even now it is this foreign language which unites all corners of this vast country.

The scheme of this book is very simple. After teaching lessons, exercises have been incorporated so that the learner learns how to form sentences of his own step by step. There is some elaboration of grammar because the basic correctness of any language lies in learning grammar.

People who shut their eyes to grammar can never write correct language. We have presented only the very important aspects of grammar so as not to load the reader with the plethora of rules but give just enough load which he can carry easily and enjoys it.

Towards the end a few pages of vocabulary have been added to give additional information on the language. It is our belief that the reader will feel the difference himself when he compares this book with those already in the market. We are always open to constructive criticism and suggestions to improve our work still further.

Author

CONTENTS

अ आ इ

ई उ ऊ

ऋ ए ऐ

ओ औ अं

अः

1

CONSONANTS

घ	ग	ख	क
ज	छ	च	ङ
झ	ट	ञ	झ
त	ण	ट	ड
न	ध	द	थ
भ	ब	द	प
ळ	र	फ	म
स	ष	य	व
ह	श	श	ह

2

Exercise

Practice writing the vowels and consonants :

आ आ इ ई उ ऊ ऋ ए ऐ
ओ औ अं अः

क	ख	ग	घ	ङ
च	छ	ज	झ	ञ
ट	ठ	ड	ढ	ण
त	थ	द	ध	न
प	फ	ब	भ	म
य	र	ल	व	
श	ष	स	ह	
	ळ	क्ष	ज्ञ	

CHAPTER 2
PRONUNCIATION

(VOWELS - स्वर)

अ (a)

Pronunciation of the letter अ (a) as the first a in the word **'Arab'**

आ (aa)

Pronunciation of the letter आ (aa) as the first a in the words like – **arc** and **arm**.

इ (i)

For the third vowel the letter इ (i) must be pronounced as first i is pronounced in the words – **is India, Iran**.

ई (ee)

This letter ई (ee) is the long pronunciation of the letter इ (i) like – **sweet, feet**.

उ (u)

For the vowel उ (u) pronounce the letter as in the words – **Urdu, push**.

ऊ (oo)

This vowel ऊ (oo) is the long pronunciation of vowel उ (u) like – **fool, stool**.

ए (e)

The vowel ए (e) should be pronounced as **e** is pronounced in the word **egg.**

ऐ (ai)

The vowel ऐ (ai) should be pronounced as **ai** in **paisa.**

ओ (o)

This letter ओ (o) should be pronounced as in the words – **open, opaque, opinion.**

औ (au)

The vowel औ (au) should be pronounced as **au** in **stout.**

अं (am)

The dot on the letter अ is pronounced as half **m** like – **humble.** It will be written in Marathi as हंबल.

अः (ah)

The two dots shown behind अ should be pronounced as **ah.**

ऋ (rv)

The vowel ऋ (rv) should be pronounced as **rv** as in नृप.

ॲ

This is used for writing foreign sounds like –
bat-बॅट, mat-मॅट, rat-रॅट.

ऑ

This letter is also used for writing foreign
sounds – **pot-पॉट, foreign-फॉरिन.**

CONSONANTS

(व्यंजने)

क्	ख्	ग्	घ्	ङ्
k	kh	g	gh	n

च्	छ्	ज्	झ्	ञ्
ch	chh	j	jh	n

ट्	ठ्	ड्	ढ्	ण्
t	th	d	dh	n

(These consonants should be pronounced by cerebral. These are called **palatal consonants**.)

त्	थ्	द्	ध्	न्
t	th	d	dh	n

प्	फ्	ब्	भ्	म्
p	ph	b	bh	m

य्	र्	ल्	व्	
y	r	l	v	

श्	ष्	स्	ह्	
sh	sh	s	h	

ळ्	क्ष्	त्र्	ज्ञ्	
la	ksh	tr	dny	

(These consonants are often used in combination of vowel अ like क्+अ=क.)

CONSONANTS WITH VOWELS

(सस्वर व्यंजने)

क	**ख**	**ग**	**घ**	**ङ**
ka	kha	ga	gha	na
च	**छ**	**ज**	**झ**	**ञ**
cha	chha	ja	jha	na
ट	**ठ**	**ड**	**ढ**	**ण**
ta	tha	da	dha	na
त	**थ**	**द**	**ध**	**न**
ta	tha	da	dha	na
प	**फ**	**ब**	**भ**	**म**
pa	pha	ba	bha	ma
य	**र**	**ल**	**व**	
ya	ra	la	va	
श	**ष**	**स**	**ह**	**ळ**
sa	sha	sa	ha	la
क्ष	**त्र**	**ज्ञ**		
ksha	tra	dna		

Exercise

Read the following :

कर, बघ, धर, धन, नथ, ढग, फळ, ऊस, कस,
पकड, मगर, भगर, दगड, मन, तन, यम, इतर,
सरबत, झटपट, पटपट, खरखट, दऊत, जग, अटक

8

SIGNS OF VOWELS
(स्वरचिह्ने)

Vowel	Sign	Usage
अ a		अजब ajab
आ aa	ा	राम Ram
इ i	ि	दिवस divas
ई ee	ी	सीता Seeta
उ u	ु	चुना chuna
ऊ oo	ू	दूध doodh
ए e	े	भेट bhet
ऐ ai	ै	पैसा paisa
ओ o	ो	पोपट popat
औ au	ौ	औत aut
अं am		अंबारी ambari
अः ah	:	पुनः punah
ऋ ru		मृग mrug

BARAKHADI
(बाराखडी)

Adding of vowels to consonants is called in **Marathi** (बाराखडी) **Barakhadi.** There are twelve main vowels, so it is called **Barakhadi.**

क	का	कि	की	कु	कू
k	ka	ki	kee	ku	koo

के	कै	को	कौ	कं	कः
ke	kai	ko	kau	kam	kah

ख	खा	खि	खी	खु	खू
kh	kha	khi	khee	khu	khoo

खे	खै	खो	खौ	खं	खः
khe	khai	kho	khau	kham	khah

ग	गा	गि	गी	गु	गू
g	ga	gi	gee	gu	goo

गे	गै	गो	गौ	गं	गः
ge	gai	go	gau	gam	gah

घ	घा	घि	घी	घु	घू
gh	gha	ghi	ghee	ghu	ghoo

घे	घै	घो	घौ	घं	घः
ghe	ghai	gho	ghou	gham	ghah

10

ङ	ङा	ङि	ङी	ङु	ङू
n	na	ni	nee	nu	noo
ङे	ङै	ङो	ङौ	ङं	ङः
ne	nai	no	nau	nam	nah
च	चा	चि	ची	चु	चू
ch	cha	chi	chee	chu	choo
चे	चै	चो	चौ	चं	चः
che	chai	cho	chau	cham	chah
छ	छा	छि	छी	छु	छू
chh	chha	chhi	chhee	chhu	chhoo
छे	छै	छो	छौ	छं	छः
chhe	chhai	chho	chhau	chham	chhah
ज	जा	जि	जी	जु	जू
j	ja	ji	jee	ju	joo
जे	जै	जो	जौ	जं	जः
je	jai	jo	jau	jam	jah
झ	झा	झि	झी	झु	झू
jh	jha	jhi	jhee	jhu	jhoo
झे	झै	झो	झौ	झं	झः
jhe	jhai	jho	jhau	jham	jhah

11

अ n	आ na	जि ni	औी nee	जु nu	जू noo
ए ne	ऐ nai	ओ no	औ nau	अं nam	अः nah
ट t	टा ta	टि ti	टी tee	टु tu	टू too
टे te	टै tai	टो to	टौ tau	टं tam	टः tah
ठ th	ठा tha	ठि thi	ठी thee	ठु thu	ठू thoo
ठे the	ठै thai	ठो tho	ठौ thau	ठं tham	ठः thah
ड d	डा da	डि di	डी dee	डु du	डू doo
डे de	डै dai	डो do	डौ dau	डं dam	डः dah
ढ dh	ढा dha	ढि dhi	ढी dhee	ढु dhu	ढू dhoo
ढे dhe	ढै dhai	ढो dho	ढौ dhan	ढं dham	ढः dhah

ण	णा	णि	णी	णु	णू
n	na	ni	nee	nu	noo
णे	णै	णो	णौ	णं	णः
ne	nai	no	nau	nam	nah
त	ता	ति	ती	तु	तू
t	ta	ti	tee	tu	too
ते	तै	तो	तौ	तं	तः
te	tai	to	tau	tam	tah
थ	था	थि	थी	थु	थू
th	tha	thi	thee	thu	thoo
थे	थै	थो	थौ	थं	थः
the	thai	tho	thau	tham	thah
द	दा	दि	दी	दु	दू
d	da	di	dee	du	doo
दे	दै	दो	दौ	दं	दः
de	dai	di	dau	dam	dah
ध	धा	धि	धी	धु	धू
dh	dha	dhi	dhee	dhu	dhoo
धे	धै	धो	धौ	धं	धः
dhe	dhai	dho	dhau	dham	dhah

13

न	ना	नि	नी	नु	नू
n	na	ni	nee	nu	noo
ने	नै	नो	नौ	नं	नः
ne	nai	no	nau	nam	nah
प	पा	पि	पी	पु	पू
p	pa	pi	pee	pu	poo
पे	पै	पो	पौ	पं	पः
pe	pai	po	pau	pam	pah
फ	फा	फि	फी	फु	फू
ph	pha	phi	phee	phu	phoo
फे	फै	फो	फौ	फं	फः
phe	phai	pho	phau	pham	phah
ब	बा	बि	बी	बु	बू
b	ba	bi	bee	bu	boo
बे	बै	बो	बौ	बं	बः
be	bai	bo	bau	bam	bah
भ	भा	भि	भी	भु	भू
bh	bha	bhi	bhee	bhu	bhoo
भे	भै	भो	भौ	भं	भः
bhe	bhai	bho	bhau	bham	bhah

म m	मा ma	मि mi	मी mee	मु mu	मू moo
मे me	मै mai	मो mo	मौ mau	मं mam	मः mah
य y	या ya	यि yi	यी yee	यु yu	यू yoo
ये ye	यै yai	यो yo	यौ yau	यं yam	यः yah
र r	रा ra	रि ri	री ree	रु ru	रू roo
रे re	रै rai	रो ro	रौ rau	रं ram	रः rah
ल l	ला la	लि li	ली lee	लु lu	लू loo
ले le	लै lai	लो lo	लौ lau	लं lam	लः lah
व v	वा va	वि vi	वी vee	वु vu	वू voo
वे ve	वै vai	वो vo	वौ vau	वं vam	वः vah

15

श	शा	शि	शी	शु	शू
sh	sha	shi	shee	shu	shoo
शे	शै	शो	शौ	शं	शः
she	shai	sho	shau	sham	shah
ष	षा	षि	षी	षु	षू
sh	sha	shi	shee	shu	shoo
षे	षै	षो	षौ	षं	षः
she	shai	sho	shau	sham	shah
स	सा	सि	सी	सु	सू
s	sa	si	see	su	soo
से	सै	सो	सौ	सं	सः
se	sai	so	sau	sam	sah
ह	हा	हि	ही	हु	हू
h	ha	hi	hee	hu	hoo
हे	है	हो	हौ	हं	हः
he	hai	ho	hau	ham	hah
ळ	ळा	ळि	ळी	ळु	ळू
l	la	li	lee	lu	loo
ळे	ळै	ळो	ळौ	ळं	ळः
le	lai	lo	lau	lam	lah

16

क्ष	**क्षा**	**क्षि**	**क्षी**	**क्षु**	**क्षू**
ksh	ksha	kshi	kshee	kshu	kshoo
क्षे	**क्षै**	**क्षो**	**क्षौ**	**क्षं**	**क्षः**
kshe	kshai	ksho	kshau	ksham	kshah
त्र	**त्रा**	**त्रि**	**त्री**	**त्रु**	**त्रू**
tr	tra	tri	tree	tru	troo
त्रे	**त्रै**	**त्रो**	**त्रौ**	**त्रं**	**त्रः**
tre	trai	tro	trau	tram	trah
ज्ञ	**ज्ञा**	**ज्ञि**	**ज्ञु**	**ज्ञू**	
dny	dnya	dnyi	dnyee	dnyu	dnyoo
ज्ञे	**ज्ञै**	**ज्ञो**	**ज्ञौ**	**ज्ञं**	**ज्ञः**
dnye	dnyai	dnyo	dnyau	dnym	dnyh

Note:- Special pronunciation of :

क, ण, ठ, द, त

पळ, दगड, माठ, बाण, ताट

Exercise

Read the following :

पकड, घार, पिवळा, धीट, गुण, ऊस, केस, ऐक,
पोट, डोल, अंबारी, पुनः, ऋषी

17

VERBS
(क्रियापदे - kriyapade)

English	Marathi	Pronunciation
eat	खा	kha
drink	पी	pee
come	ये	ye
go	जा	ja
give	दे	de
wash	धू	dhoo
sing	गा	ga
keep	ठेव	thev
hear	ऐक	aik
listen	लक्ष दे	laksha de
read	वाच	vach
cut	काप	kap
sleep	झोप	jhop
come on	चल	chal
speak	बोल	bol
say	म्हण	mhan
tell	सांग	sang
apply	लाव	lav
do	कर	kar
climb up	चढ	chadh
run	पळ	pal
leave	सोड	sod
take out	काढ	kadh
stay	रहा	raha

18

English	Marathi		Pronunciation
look	बघ)	same	bagh
see	पहा)	meaning	paha
beat	मार		mar
kill	मार		mar
drive	चालव		chalav
hold	धर		dhar
open	उघड		ughad
shut	बंद कर		band kar
close	बंद कर		band kar
fill	भर		bhar
fetch	घेऊन ये		gheoon ye
take with you	घेऊन जा		gheoon ja
take	घे		ghe
sweep	झाडु मार		jhadu mar
send	पाठव		pathav
climb down	उतर		utar
stop	थांब		thamb
show	दाखव		dakhav
put on the light	दिवा लाव		diva lav
put off the light	दिवा मालव		diva malav
become	बन (हो)		ban (ho)
is	आहे		ahe
fall down	पड		pad

19

English	Marathi	Pronunciation
are	आहेत	ahet
was	होता	hota
were	होते	hote
will be	(होईल) होतील	(hoeel) hoteel

Pronouns

I	मी	mee
you	तू	too
he	तो	to
that	ते	te
she	ती	tee
we	आम्ही	amhi
you (pl)	तुम्ही	tumhi
)	ते *masculine*	(te
they)	त्या *feminine*	(tya
)	ती *neuter*	(tee

20

WORDS OF TWO LETTERS
(दोन अक्षरी शब्द - don akshri shabad)

Marathi	English	Pronunciation
अधू	weak	adhoo
अधु	weak, deformed	adhu
एक	one	ek
कडू	bitter	kadu
काम	work	kam
गाडी	car, motor	gadi
केव्हा	when	kevha
नाव	name	nav
नाव	boat	nav
शाई	ink	shai
साप	snake	sap
पूर्व	east	poorva
वर	up, on	var
खाली	down, below	khali
बाजू	side	baju
आत	in, inside	aat
मागे	behind	mage
मध्ये	inside	madhye
चित्र	picture	chitra
झाड	tree	jhad
आज	today	aaj
उद्या	tomorrow	udya
काल	yesterday	kaal

Marathi	English	Pronunciation
कवि	poet	kavi
नदी	river	nadi
देश	country	desh
रोज	everyday	roj
पुन्हा	again	punha
पण	but	pun
बरं	O.K.	baran
काय	what	kay
कुठे	where	kuthe
कोण	who	kon
कोणचं	which	konchn
जर	if	jar
तर	then	tar
आणि	and	ani
खूप	very	khoop
फार	very	phar
सध्या	now-a-days	sadhya
पूर्ण	complete	purn
अर्ध	half	ardh
आधी	first, before	adhi
तार	wire	tar
पेटी	box	petee
चहा	tea	chaha
कॉफी	coffee	cofee
इथे	here	ithe

Marathi	English	Pronunciation
तिथे	there	tithe
खडू	chalk	khadu
ढग	cloud	dhag
पाणी	water	pani
गाय	cow	gay

WORDS OF THREE LETTERS
(तीन अक्षरी शब्द –teen akshri shabad)

Marathi	English	Pronunciation
समुद्र	sea	samudra
उजेड	light	ujed
प्रकाश	light	prakash
अंधार	darkness	andhar
गवत	grass	gavat
कपडे	clothes	kapade
सदरा	shirt	sadara
धोतर	a male garment a dhoti	dhotar
पातळ, साडी	sari	patal, sadi
पातळ	thin, liquid	patal
लुगडे	sari	lugade
गडद	dark	gadad
कापड	cloth	kapad
चादर	bedsheet	chadar
फडके	a piece of cloth	phadake
पश्चिम	west	paschim

23

Marathi	English	Pronunciation
उत्तर	north	uttar
दक्षिण	south	dakshin
आग्नेय	east-south	agneya
वायव्य	south-west	vayavya
नैऋत्य	west-north	nairutya
ईशान्य	north-east	ishanya
भारत	India	Bharat
माणूस, मानव	man	manoos
अजून	still	ajun
इकडे	here	ikade
तिकडे	there	tikade
कागद	page	kagad
लेखणी	pen	lekhani
दिवस	day	divas
फुकट	waste, free	phukat
चटई	mat	chatai
औषध	medicine	aushadha
पलंग	bed	palang
चप्पल	sandal	chappal
अपूर्ण	incomplete	apurn
क्वचित्	rarely	kwachit
किंचित	a little	kinchit
आरसा	mirror	arasa
कलम	graft	kalam
कलम करणे	to cut	kalam karane

Marathi	English	Pronunciation
जवळ	near	jawal
हसणे	to laugh	hasane
रडणे	to cry	radane
नाचणे	to dance	nachane
बांगडी	bangle	bangadi
अंगठी	ring	angathi
पुतळा	a statue	putala
रुमाल	handkerchief	rumal
सवय	habit	savay
हृदय	heart	hruday
पाऊस	rain	paus
आकाश	sky	akash
अजून	still	ajun
कारण	because	karan
उगीच	unnecessarily	ugeech
नंतर	then, afterwards	nantar
म्हणून	therefore	mhanoon
परंतु	but	parantu
तसेच	similarly	tasech
विमान	aeroplane	viman
ज्योतिष	astrology	jyotish
दैनिक	daily	dainik
मासिक	monthly	masik
वार्षिक	yearly	varshik

WORDS OF FOUR LETTERS
(चार अक्षरी शब्द – char akshri shabad)

Marathi	English	Pronunciation
आगगाडी	railway	aag gadie
आगपेटी	matchbox	aag petee
सावकाश	slowly	savakash
लवकर	early	lavakar
चटकंन	quickly	chatakan
साप्ताहिक	weekly	saptahik
सोमवार	Monday	somvar
मंगळवार	Tuesday	mangalvar
बुधवार	Wednesday	budhavar
गुरुवार	Thursday	guruvar
शुक्रवार	Friday	shukravar
शनिवार	Saturday	shanivar
रविवार	Sunday	rvivar
ग्रंथालय	library	granthalaya
वाचनालय	reading hall	vachnalay
उपहारगृह	restaurant	upahargruh
रसवंतीगृह	juice house	rasvantigruh
विद्यापीठ	university	vidyapith
नाटकगृह	theatre	natakgruh
वस्तु संग्राहलय	museum	vastu sangrahlay
प्राणी संग्राहलय	zoo	prani sangrahalay
विमानतळ	aerodrome	vimantal
स्थानक	station	sthanak
नगरपालिका	municipality	nagarpalika

Chapter 3
CLASSIFIED NAMES

Relation (नाती - nati)
Relatives (नातेवाईक - natevaik)

English	Marathi	Pronunciation
mother	आई	aai
father	वडील	vadeel
sister	बहीण	baheen
brother	भाऊ	bhaoo
grandfather	आजोबा	aajoba
grandmother	आजी	aajee
uncle (paternal)	काका	kaka
aunt (paternal)	आत्या	atya
aunt	काकू (काकी)	kaku (kakee)
uncle (maternal)	मामा	mama
aunt (maternal)	मावशी	mavashee
aunt (maternal)	मामी	mamee
grandson	नातू	natu
granddaughter	नात	nat
father-in-law	सासरा	saasara
mother-in-law	सासू	sasoo

English	Marathi	Pronunciation
brother-in-law	मेहुणा, दीर	mehuna, deer
sister-in-law	मेहुणी, नणंद	mehunee, nanand
husband	पति	pati
wife	पत्नी	patni
son	मुलगा	mulaga
daughter	मुलगी	mulagi
unmarried	अविवाहित	avivahit
man	पुरुष	purush
woman	महिला, स्त्री, बाई	mahila, stree, bai
son-in-law	जावई	javai
daughter-in-law	सून	soon (sun)
relation	नाते	nate
Mr.	श्री	sree
Mrs.	श्रीमती	sreemati
Miss	कुमारी	kumari
master	कुमार	kumar
elder	मोठा	motha
younger	छोटा	chota

COLOUR
(रंग – rang)

English	Marathi	Pronunciation
red	लाल, ताम्बडा	lal, tambda
blue	निळा	nila
yellow	पिवळा	pivala
violet	जांभळा	jambhala

English	Marathi	Pronunciation
green	हिरवा	hirava
orange	केशरी, नारंगी	keshari, narangi
white	पांढरा	pandhra
black	काळा	kala
pink	गुलाबी	gulabi
brown	भुरा, चॉकलेटी, तपकिरी	bhura, chocleti, tapkiri
grey	करडा, राखाडी	karada, rakhadi
mixed	मिश्र	mishra
deep, dark	गडद	gadad
pale	फिकट	phikat
-ish	–सर	-sar

Example :

greyish	राखडीसर	rakhdisar
many-hued	चित्रविचित्र	chitra vichitra

FRUITS
(फळें - falain)

English	Marathi	Pronunciation
mango	आंबा	amba
banana	केळं	keln
apple	सफरचंद	sapharchand
orange	संत्रे	santre
grapes	द्राक्षे	drakshe
guava	पेरू	peru
pineapple	अननस	ananas
jackfruit	फणस	phanas

English	Marathi	Pronunciation
sweetlime	मुसुंबी	musumbi
custard apple	सीताफळ	seetaphal
pomegranate	डाळिंब	dalimb
flagon	जांब	jamb
jamun	जांभूळ	jambhool
Indian plum	बोर	bor
pummelo	पपनस	papanas
chiku	चिक्कू	chikku
date	खजूर	khajoor
plums	आलुबुखार	alubukhar
water melon	कलिंगड	kalingad
corinda	करवंद	karavand
papaya	पपई	papai
peach	आडू	aadu
coconut	नारळ	naral
stone apple	कवठ	kawath
mulberry	तूती	tuti
emblic myrobolan	आवळा	avala
lemon	लिंबू	limboo

FLOWERS
(फुले - phole)

English	Marathi	Pronunciation
rose	गुलाब	gulab
jasmine	चमेली, मोगरा	chameli, mogra
lotus	कमळ	kamal

English	Marathi	Pronunciation
shoe flower, china rose	जास्वंद	jaswand
sunflower	सूर्यफूल	soorya phool
champak	चाफा	chapha
bud	कळी	kalee
blossom	मोहोर	mohar
lily	लिली	lilee
tagar	तगर	tagar (a type of white flower)
	मधुमालती	madhumalti
	शेवंती	shevanti
tube rose	निशिगंध	nishigandh
	रातराणी	ratrani
	बकुळ	bakul
yellow amaranth	अबोली	aboli
butterfly pea	गोकर्ण	gokarna
goldmohar	गुलमोहर	gulmohar
lantana	घाणेरी	ghaneri
marvel of peru or four o'clock plant	गुलबक्षी	gulbakshi
oleander	कण्हेर	kanher
night jasmin	पारिजातक	parijatak
screw pine	केवडा	kewada
passion flower	कृष्णकमळ	krishan kamal

VEGETABLES

(भाज्या-bhajya)

English	Marathi	Pronunciation
radish	मुळा	mula
cabbage	कोबी	kobee
cauliflower	फुलकोबी	phulkobi
chilli	मिरची	mirchee
cucumber	काकडी	kakadi
ladyfinger	भेंडी	bhendi
onion	कांदा	kanda
peas	मटार	matar
potato	बटाटा	batata
pumpkin	लालभोपळा	lal bhopala
carrot	गाजर	gajar
snake gourd	पडवळ	padwal
tomato	टोमॅटो	tomato
lemon	लिंबू	limbu
peas	वाटाणे	vatane
beans	वाल	val
bottle gourd	दुधी भोपळा	dudhi bhopala
garlic	लसूण	lasoon
ginger	आले	aalen
ribbed gourd	दोडके	dodake
bath sponge or loofah	घोसाळे	ghosale
bitter gourd	कारले	karle

32

ARTICLES OF FOOD

(खाण्याचे पदार्थ - khanyache padartha)

English	Marathi	Pronunciation
cereal	धान्य	dhanya
wheat	गहू	gahu
rice	तांदूळ	tandul
pulse	डाळ	dal
pearl millet	बाजरी	bajri
maize	मका	maka
green gram	मूग	mug
black gram	उडीद	udid
butter	लोणी	loni
buttermilk	ताक	tak
curd	दही	dahi
salt	मीठ	meeth
pungent	तिखट	tikhat
turmeric	हळद	halad
tamarind	चिंच	chinch
sugar	साखर	sakhar
jaggery	गूळ	gul
cumin seeds	जिरे	jire
mustard	मोहरी	mohari
cardamom	वेलदोडे	veldode
groundnut	भुईमुगाचे दाणे	bhuimugache dane
black pepper	काळी मिरी	kali miri

English	Marathi	Pronunciation
spice	मसाला	masala
meat	मांस	mansa
egg	अंडे	ande
fish	मासे	mase

SEASONS AND WEATHER
(ऋतु आणि हवामान – ritu ani havaman)

English	Marathi	Pronunciation
spring	वसंत	vasant
summer	ग्रीष्म	greeshma
rainy season	वर्षा	varsha
autumn	शरद	sharad
winter	हेमंत	hemant
	शिशिर	shishir
wind, breeze	वारा	vara
air	हवा	hava
lightning	वीज	veej
rain	पाऊस	paoos
cloud	ढग	dhag
storm	वादळ	vadal
thunder	मेघगर्जना	meghgarjana
flood	पूर	poor
cold	थंडी	thandi
hot	गरम, उष्ण	garam, ushan

34

MINERALS AND ALLOYS

(खनिजे - khanije)

English	Marathi	Pronunciation
gold	सोने	sone
silver	चांदी	chandi
iron	लोखंड	lokhand
coal	कोळसा	kolsa
steel	पोलाद	polad
brass	पितळ	pital
copper	तांबे	tambe
lead	शिसे	shise
metal	धातु	dhatu
diamond	हिरा	hira
ruby	माणिक	manik
emerald	पाचु	pachu
pearl	मोती	moti
coral	पोवळे	povale
zink	जस्त	jasta
mica	अभ्रक	abhrak

FEELINGS

(भावना - bhavana)

(I)

English	Marathi	Pronunciation
joy	आनंद	anand
sorrow	दुःख	duhkha
pleasure	सुख	sukh

English	Marathi	Pronunciation
anger	राग	rag
hate	द्वेष	dvesh
love	प्रेम	prem
jealousy	मत्सर	matsar
pity	दया	daya
doubt	शंका	shanka
fear	भीती	bheeti
laughter	हास्य	hasya
hope	आशा	asha
weep, cry	रडू	radu
greed	हाव	haav
friendship	मैत्री	maitri
temptation	मोह	moha
enmity	शत्रुता	shatruta

(II)

Marathi	English	Pronunciation
आनंद	आनंदी (happy)	anandi
दुःख	दुःखी (sad)	dukhi
सुख	सुखी (happy)	sukhi
राग	रागीट (angry)	rageet
द्वेष	द्वेषी (hostile)	dveshi
प्रेम	प्रेमळ (loving)	premal
मत्सर	मत्सरी (jealous)	matsaree
दया	दयाळू (kind)	dayaloo

36

Marathi	English	Pronunciation
शंका	शंकेखोर (doubter)	shankekhor
भीती	भित्रा (coward)	bhitra
हास्य	हसरा (smiling)	hasra
आशा	आशावादी (optimist)	ashavadee
रडू	रडवा, रडका (given to cry)	radva, radka
हाव	हावरट (greedy)	havrat
मैत्री	मित्र (friend)	mitre

POST
(टपाल -tapal)

English	Marathi	Pronunciation
post office	टपालकचेरी	tapal kacheri
delivery	वितरण	vitaran
letter	पत्र	patra
envelop	पाकिट	pakit
inland	अंतर्देशीय	antardeshiye
stamp	तिकिट	tikit
address	पत्ता	patta
cancellation mark	शिक्का	shikka
reply	उत्तर	uttar
parcel	पार्सल	parcel
telegram	तार	tar
moneyorder	मनिऑर्डर	moneyorder
postmaster	पोस्ट मास्तर	postmaster
postman	पत्रवाहक	patravahak

WORK
(काम – kam)

English	Marathi	Pronunciation
business	धंदा	dhanda
factory, workshop	कारखाना	karkhana
industry	उद्योग	udyog
employer	मालक	malak
labourer	मजूर, कामगार	majoor, kamgar
servant	नोकर	nokar
manager	प्रबंधक	prabandhak
clerk	लिपिक	lipik
accountant	अकाउंटंट	accountant
typist	टायपिस्ट (लेखनिक)	lekhanik
salary	पगार, वेतन	pagar, vetan
office	कचेरी, कार्यालय	kacheree, karyalay
dearness allowance	महागाई भत्ता	mahagai bhatta
wages	मजुरी	majuree
insurance	विमा	vima
bank	संचयिका	sanchayika

NEWS
(वार्ता - **varta**)

English	*Marathi*	*Pronunciation*
newspaper	वृत्त पत्र	vrutta patra
press	छापखाना	chapakhana
reporter	वार्ताहर	vartahar
author	लेखक	lekhak
daily	दैनिक	dainik
monthly	मासिक	masik
weekly	साप्ताहिक	saptahik
fortnightly	पाक्षिक	pakshik
television	दूरदर्शन	doordarshan
radio	आकाशवाणी	aakashvani
telephone	दूरध्वनी	doordhwani

MEASURES
(माप - **map**)

English	*Marathi*	*Pronunciation*
measure	माप	map
weight	वजन	vajan
kilo	किलो	kilo
metre	मीटर	mitar
length	लांबी	lambi
height	उंची	unchi

English	Marathi	Pronunciation
breadth	रुंदी	rundi
litre	लिटर	litar
a little	थोडे	thode
correct	बरोबर	barobar
more, much	जास्त	jast
inches	इंच	inch
centimetre	सेंटीमीटर	sentimetar

INSECTS
(कीटक - **kitak**)

English	Marathi	Pronunciation
lizzard	पाल	pal
fly	माशी	mashi
mosquito	डास	daas
cockroach	झुरळ	jhural
bug	ढेकूण	dhekun
bee	मधमाशी	madhmashi
ant	मुंगी	mungi
spider	कोळी	koli
white ant	वाळवी	valavi
worm	कृमी	krumi
gadfly	गांधीलमाशी	gandhilmashi
earthworm	गांडुळ	gandul

NUMERALS
(संख्याविचार)

१	एक	ek	1
२	दोन	don	2
३	तीन	teen	3
४	चार	char	4
५	पाच	pach	5
६	सहा	saha	6
७	सात	saat	7
८	आठ	aath	8
९	नऊ	nau	9
१०	दहा	dahaa	10
११	अकरा	akara	11
१२	बारा	bara	12
१३	तेरा	tera	13
१४	चौदा	chauda	14
१५	पंधरा	pandhara	15
१६	सोळा	sola	16

41

१७	सतरा	satra	17
१८	अठरा	athara	18
१९	एकोणीस	ekonis	19
२०	वीस	wis	20
२१	एक्वीस	ekwis	21
२२	बावीस	bawis	22
२३	तेवीस	tewis	23
२४	चोवीस	chowis	24
२५	पंचवीस	pachwis	25
२६	सव्वीस	savwis	26
२७	सत्तावीस	sattawis	27
२८	अट्ठावीस	atthawis	28
२९	एकोणतीस	ekontis	29
३०	तीस	tis	30
३१	एकतीस	ektis	31
३२	बत्तीस	battis	32
३३	तेहतीस	tehtis	33
३४	चौतीस	chautis	34
३५	पस्तीस	pastis	35
३६	छत्तीस	chattis	36
३७	सदतीस	sadatis	37
३८	अडतीस	adatis	38
३९	एकोणचाळीस	akonchalis	39
४०	चाळीस	chalis	40
४१	एक्केचाळीस	ekkechalis	41
४२	बेचाळीस	bechalis	42

42

४३	त्रेचाळीस	trechalis	43
४४	चौवेचाळीस	chovlechalis	44
४५	पंचेचाळीस	panchechalis	45
४६	सेहेचाळीस	sehechalis	46
४७	सत्तेचाळीस	sattechalis	47
४८	अट्ठेचाळीस	atthechalis	48
४९	एकोणपन्नास	ekonpannas	49
५०	पन्नास	pannas	50
५१	एक्कावन	ekkavanna	51
५२	बावन	bavanna	52
५३	त्रेपन्न	trepanna	53
५४	चोपन्न	chopanna	54
५५	पंचावन	panchavanna	55
५६	छप्पन	chappanna	56
५७	सत्तावन	sattavanna	57
५८	अट्ठावन	atthavanna	58
५९	एकोणसाठ	ekonsath	59
६०	साठ	sath	60
६१	एकसष्ठ	eksaahtha	61
६२	बासष्ठ	basashtha	62
६३	त्रेसष्ठ	tresashtha	63
६४	चौसष्ठ	chousashtha	64
६५	पासष्ठ	pasashtha	65
६६	सहासष्ठ	sahasashtha	66
६७	सदुसष्ठ	sadusashtha	67
६८	अडुसष्ठ	adusashtha	68

६९	एकोणसत्तर	ekonsattar	69
७०	सत्तर	sattar	70
७१	एक्काहत्तर	ekkahattar	71
७२	बहात्तर	bahattar	72
७३	त्र्यहत्तर	tryhattar	73
७४	चौऱ्याहत्तर	chouryahattar	74
७५	पंचाहत्तर	panchyahattar	75
७६	शहात्तर	shahattar	76
७७	सत्याहत्तर	sattyahattar	77
७८	अद्याहत्तर	athyahattar	78
७९	एकोणऐंशी	ekonainshee	79
८०	ऐंशी	ainshee	80
८१	एक्याऐंशी	ekyaainshee	81
८२	ब्याऐंशी	byaainshee	82
८३	त्र्याऐंशी	traainshee	83
८४	चौऱ्याऐंशी	chouryaainshee	84
८५	पंच्याऐंशी	panchyaainshee	85
८६	शहाऐंशी	shahaainshee	86
८७	सत्याऐंशी	satyaainshee	87
८८	अद्याऐंशी	athyaainshee	88
८९	एकोणनव्वद	ekonnavvaad	89
९०	नव्वद	navvad	90
९१	एक्याण्णव	ekyannav	91
९२	ब्याण्णव	byannav	92
९३	त्र्याण्णव	tryannav	93
९४	चौऱ्याण्णब	chouryannav	94

Chapter 4
TRANSLATION

LESSON 1
(धडा 1 - dhada 1)

आई, कमळ बघ – Mother, see the lotus.

कमळ छान आहे – The lotus is beautiful.

कमळ लाल आहे – The lotus is red.

आई, मला कमळ दे – Mother, give me the lotus.

Words :

आई = mother = aai

अ + ा = आ (aa)
       ई (ee) = आई

कमळ = lotus = kamal
    क् + अ = क (k) म् + अ = म (m) ळ् + अ = ळ
    (l) = कमळ

बघ = see = bagh
    ब् + अ = ब (b) घ् + अ = घ (gh) = बघ

लाल ∵ red = lal
    ल् + अ + ा = ला (la) ल् + अ = ल (l) = लाल

आहे = is = aahe *(present tense)*

छान = beautiful, good = chan

    छ् + अ + ा = छा (chha) न् + अ + न = छान

मला = me = mala

    म् + अ = म (m) ल् + अ + ा = ला (la) = मला

दे = give = de

    द् + ए = दे (de) = दे

LESSON 2
(घडा 2 – dhada 2)

मला पाणी दे – Give me water.

मला थंड पाणी दे – Give me cold water.

मी पाणी गिळले – I swallow the water.

मुकुंद, दिवा लाव – Mukund, switch on the light.

Words :

पाणी = water = pani

    पा = प् + आ = पा (pa)

    णी = ण् + ई (ी) = णी (ni) = पाणी

थंड = cold = thand

    थं = थ् + अ + न् = थं (than) *(half n)*

    ड = ड् + अ = ड (d) = थंड

गिळले = swallow = gilale

    गि = ग् + इ (ि) = गि (gi)

    ळ = ळ् + अ = ळ (l)

    ले = ल् + ए (े) = ले (lai) = गिळले

मुकुंद = This is a male name.

    मु = म् + उ (ु) = मु (mu)

    कुं = क् + उ (ु) + न् = कुं (kun) *(half n)*

    द = द् + अ = द (d) = मुकुंद

48

दिवा – light – diva

    दि = द् + इ (ि) = दि (di)

    वा = व् + आ (ा) = वा (va) = दिवा

लाव = light = lav

लावणे – to light = lavane

    ला = ल् + आ (ा) = ला

    व = व् + अ = व (v) = लाव

    खिडकी लाव – Close the window.

Here the word लाव is used, meaning 'close'.

LESSON 3

(धडा ३ - dhada 3)

मी शाळेत जातो – I go to school.

शाळेत मुले येतात – Boys come to school.

शाळेत मुली येतात – Girls come to school.

शाळेत बाई येतात – Madam comes to school.
Madams come to school.

मला शाळा फार आवडते – I like school very much.

Words :

मी = I – mee

मी = म् + ई (ी) = मी

शाळेत = to school, in a school – shalet

शा = श् + अ + ा = शा (sha)

ळे = ळ् + ए (े) = ळे (le)

त = त् + अ = त (t) = शाळेत

जातो = go – jato

जा = ज् + आ = जा (ja)

तो = त् + ओ = तो (to) = जातो

मुले = boys = mulen (*plural of* मुलगा **mulga = boy**)

मु = म् + उ (ु) = मु (mu)

ले = ल् + ए = े = ले (le) = मुले

50

येतात = come = yetat

    ये = य् + ए + ` = ये (ye)

    ता = त् + आ = ता (ta)

    त = त् + अ = त (t) = येतात

मुली = girls = mulee

    मुं = म् + उ (‿) = मु (mu)

    ली = ल् + ई (ी) = ली (lee) = मुली

बाई = madam (teacher) = bai

    बा = ब् + आ (ा) = बा (ba)

    ई = ई (ee) = बाई

मला = me = mala

    म = म् + अ = म (m)

    ला = ल् + आ = ला (la) = मला

शाळा = school = sala

    शा = श् + आ (ा) = शा (sha)

    ळा = ळ् + आ (ा) = ळा (la) = शाळा

फार = very much = phar

    फा = फ् + आ (ा) = फा (pha)

    र = र् + अ = र (r) = फार

आवडते = like = avadate

    आ = अ् + आ (ा) = आ (aa)

    व = व् + अ = व (v)

    ड = ड् + अ = ड (d)

    ते = त् + ए (े) = ते (te) = आवडते

51

LESSON 4

(धडा 4 - dhada 4)

दादा दार उघड – Brother, open the door.

ताई पिशवी उचल – Sister, take the basket.

ताई पिशवीतून भाजी काढ – Sister, take out the vegetable
from the basket.

बाळाला फुगा दे – Give the balloon to the baby.

Words :

दादा = elder brother = dada

  दा = द् + आ (ा) = दा (da)

  दा = द + आ (ा) = दा (de) = दादा

ताई = elder sister = tai

  ता = त् + आ (ा) = ता (ta)

  ई = ई (i) = ताई

दार = door = dar

  दा = द् + आ (ा) = दा (da)

  र = र् + अ = र (r) = दार

उघड = open = ughad

  उ = उ (u)

  घ = घ् + अ = घ (gh)

  ड = ड् + अ = ड (d) = उघड

पिशवी = basket = pishavee

    पि = प + इ (ि) = पि (pi)

    श = श् + अ = श (sh)

    वी = व् + ई (ी) = वी (vee) = पिशवी

उचल = off take = uchal

    उ = उ (u)

    च = च् + अ = च (ch)

    ल = ल् + अ = ल (l) = उचल

बाळाला = बाळ = a baby

    बाळाला - to the baby - balala

    बा – ब् + आ (ा) = बा (ba)

    ळा – ळ् + आ (ा) = ळा (la)

    ला – ल् + आ (ा) = ला (la) = बाळाला

फुगा = balloon = phuga

    फु – फ् + उ (ु) = फु (phu)

    गा – ग् + आ (ा) = गा (ga) = फुगा

LESSON 5
(धडा 5 - dhada 5)

बाळ उठ – Bal get up.

अंग धू – Wash the body (wash *your* body).

हात धू – Wash your hands (*arms*).

पाय धू – Wash your feet.

डोळे धू – Clean your eyes.

नाक पूस – Wipe your nose.

कान साफ कर – Clean your ears.

दात साफ कर – Wash your teeth.

केस नीट कर – Comb your hair.

बाळ – **Bal** means 'small baby' but here it is used as name.

Words :

ऊठ = get up = ooth

    ऊ = ऊ (oo)

    ट् + अ = ठ (th) = ऊठ

अंग = body = ang (शरीर – shareer)

    अं = अं (an)

    ग = ग् + अ = ग (g) = अंग

धू = wash = dhoo

धुणे = to wash = dhune

    धू = धू + ऊ (ू) = धू (dhoo)

हात = hand *or* hands - hat

    हा = ह् + आ (ा) = हा (ha)

    त = त् + अ = त (t) = हात

पाय = foot *or* feet = pay

    पा = प् + आ (ा) = पा (pa)

    य = य् + अ = य (y) = पाय

डोळे = eyes = dole (डोळा – an eye - dola)

    डो = ड् + ओ (ो) = डो (do)

    ळे = ळ् + ए (े) = ळे (le) = डोळे

नाक = nose = nak

    ना = न् + आ (ा) = ना (na)

    क = क् + अ = क (k) = नाक

पूस = wipe (It is used with nose.)

पुसणे = to wipe - pusane (poos)

    पू = प् + ऊ (ू) = पू (poo)

    स = स् + अ = स (s) = पूस

कान = an ear *or* ears = kan

    का = क् + आ (ा) = का (ka)

    न – न् + अ = न (n) = कान

साफ कर = clean = saph kar

साफ करणे = to clean = saph karne

सा = स् + आ (ा) = सा (sa)

फ = फ् + अ = फ (ph) = साफ

क = क् + अ = क (k)

र = र् + अ = र (r) = कर

दात = tooth *or* teeth = dat

दा = द् + आ (ा) = दा (da)

त = त् + अ = त (t) = दात

केस = hair = kes

के = क् + ए (े) = के (ke)

स = स् + अ = स (s) = केस

नीट कर = neat (do well) = neet

नी – न् + ई (ी) = नी (nee)

ट – ट् + अ = ट (t) = नीट

LESSON 6
(धडा 6 - dhada 6)

चेहरा दाखव – Show your face.

कपाळ दाखव – Show your forehead.

गाल दाखव – Show your cheek.

हनुवटी बघू – Let me see your chin.

जीभ बाहेर काढ – Show me your tongue.

मान वळव – Turn you neck.

कंबर वाकव – Bend your waist.

बोटं बघू – Let me see your fingers.

अंगठा बघू – Let me see your thumb.

नखं दाखव – Show your nails.

ओठ दाखव – Show your lips.

तोंड उघड – Open your mouth.

पाठ कर – Turn your back.

भुवया दाखव – Show your eyebrows.

छाती दाखव – Show your chest.

कातडी दाखव – Show your skin.

पापण्या मीट – Close your eyelids.

डोके दाखव – Show your head.

Words :

चेहरा = face = chehara

    चे = च् + ए (ॆ) = चे (che)

    ह = ह् + अ = ह (h)

    रा = र् + आ (ा) = रा (ra) = चेहरा

दाखव = show – dakhav

    दा = द् + आ (ा) = दा (da)

    ख = ख् + अ = ख (v) – दाखव

कपाळ = forehead = kapal

    क = क् + अ = क (k)

    पा = प् + आ (ा) = पा (pa)

    ळ = ळ् + अ = ळ (l) = कपाळ

गाल = cheek *or* cheeks = gal

    गा = ग् + आ (ा) = गा (ga)

    ल = ल् + अ = ल (l) = गाल

हनुवटी = chin = hanuvatee

    नु = न् + उ (ु) = नु (nu)

    टी = ट् + ई (ी) = टी (tee)

बघू = let see = baghu

    घू = घ् + ऊ (ू) = घू (ghu)

जीभ = tongue = jeebh

    जी = ज् + ई (ी) = जी (ge)

    भ = भ् + अ = जीभ

मान = neck = man

वळव = turn = valav

वळविणे = to turn = valavine

कंबर = waist = kamber

कं = कृ + अं = कं

वाकव = bent = vakav

वाकवणे = to be bent = vakavane

वाकणे = to bend = vakane

बोटं = fingers = botn (*n* is silent)

बोट = a finger = bot

अंगठा = thumb = angatha

अं = अं

नखं = nails = nakhan (last *n* is silent)

नख = a nail = nakh

ओठ = lips *or* lip = oth

तोंड = mouth = tond

तों = तृ + ओ (ो) + न् (ँ)

उघड = open = ughad

पाठ = back = path

कर = do = kar

Here in this sentence (पाठ कर) कर is used for turn.

भुवया = eyebrows = buhvaya

भुवई = an eyebrow = bhuvai

59

छाती = chest = chhati

    छा = छ् + आ (ा) = छा (cha)

    ती = त् + ई (ी) = ती (ti) = छाती

कातडी = skin = katadi

त्वचा = skin = tvacha

    त्व = त् + व् + अ = त्व (tva)

    चा = च् + आ (ा) = चा (cha) = त्वचा

पापण्या = eyelids = papanya

पापणी = an eyelid = papani

    पा = प् + आ (ा) = पा (pa)

    प = प् + अ = प (p)

    ण्या = ण् + य् + आ (ा) = ण्या (nya) = पापण्या

मीट = close = meet

डोके = head = doke

    डो = ड् + ओ (ो) = डो

    के = क् + ए (े) = के (ke) = डोके

LESSON 7
(धडा 7 – dhada 7)

ते माझे घर आहे.

That is my house.

घरात चार खोल्या आहेत.

There are four rooms in the house.

प्रत्येक खोलीला एक दरवाजा आहे.

There is one door in every room.

आम्ही भिंतींना निळा रंग दिला आहे.

We coloured our walls blue.

दिखवाणखान्याला दोन खिडक्या आहेत.

The Drawingroom has two windows.

आमच्या घरात एक संडास व एक नहाणीघर आहे.

There is a latrine and a bathroom in our house.

आमचे स्वयंपाकघर मोठे आहे.

Our kitchen is big.

घरा समोर आंगण आहे.

There is a courtyard in front of our house.

घराचं छत कौलारु आहे.

The roof of our house is tiled.

घरा समोर बाग आहे.

There is a garden in front of our house.

बाग सुंदर आहे.

The garden is beautiful.

Words :

ते = that = te

माझे = my = majhe

    झे = झ् + ए (े) = झे

घर = house = ghar

घरात = in the house = gharat

घरी = in the house, to the house = ghari

चार = four = char

खोल्या = rooms = kholya

खोली = a room = kholee

    ल्या = ल् + य् + आ (ा) = ल्या

आहेत = are = ahet

प्रत्येक = every = pratyek

    प्र = प् + र् + अ = प्र (pra)

    त्य = त् + य् + ए (े) = त्ये (tye)

    क = क् + अ = क (k) = प्रत्येक

आम्ही = we = amhee

    आ = आ

    म्ही = म् + ह् + ई (ी) = म्ही (mhee) = आम्ही

भिंतींना – to the wall – bhintinna

भिंत – wall = bhint

भिंतीत, भिंती मध्ये = in the wall

निळा = blue = nila

रंग = colour = rang

दिला = give = dila

रंग दिला आह = coloured

दिवाणखान्याला = to the drawing room = diwankhanyala

दिवाणखाना = drawing room

दिवाणखान्यात = in the drawing room

न्या = न् + य् + आ (ा) = न्या (nya)

दोन = two = don

खिडक्या = windows = khidkya

क्या = क् + य् + आ (ा) = क्या

खिडकी = a window = khidki

घरात = in the house = ghart

एक = one = ek

संडास = a privy, latrine, lavatory = sandas

व = and = v

आणि = and = ani

63

नहाणीघर = bathroom = nahanighar

स्वयंपाकघर = kitchen = swayampakghar

स्व = स् + व् + अ = स्व (swa, sva)

मोठे = big = mothe

मो = म् + ओ (ो) = मो

ठे = ठ् + ए (े) = ठ = मोठे (mothe)

समोर = in front of = samor

अंगण = courtyard = angan

घराचं = of house – gharachn (n is silent)

छत = roof = chat

कौलारू = tiled = kaularu

कौ = क् + औ (ौ) = कौ (kau)

रू = र् + ऊ (ू) = रू (ru) = कौलारू

बाग = garden = bag

सुंदर = beautiful = sundar

LESSON 8

(धडा 8 – dhada 8)

ही माझी खोली आहे – This is my room.

हे माझे कपाट आहे – This is my cupboard.

कपाटात मी पुस्तक ठेवतो – I keep books in the cupboard.

हे माझे मेज आहे – This is my table.

ही माझी खुर्ची आहे – This is my chair.

हे माझे घडयाळ आहे – This is my watch.

मोठं घडयाळ दिवाणखान्यात आहे –The clock is in the
drawing-room.

हा माझा पलंग आहे – This is my bed.

माझी = my = majhi

माझें = my = majhe

कपाट = cupboard = kapat

कपाटातं = in the cupboard = kapatat

पुस्तकें = books = pustakain

    पु = प् + उ (‿) – पु (pu)

    स्त = स् + त् + अ = स्त (sta)

    क = क् + अ = क (k) = पुस्तक

ठेवतो = keep = thevato (*masculine gender*)

ठेवते = keep = thevate

हा, हे, ही = this

मेज = table = mej

खुर्ची = chair = khurchi

> ख = ख् + उ (‗) = खु (khu)
>
> र्ची = र् + च् + ई (ी) = र्ची (rchi) = खुर्ची

घडयाळ - watch, clock = ghadyal

> घ = घ् + अ = घ (gha)
>
> डय = ड् + य् + आ (ा) = डया (dya)
>
> ळ = ळ् + अ = ळ = घडयाळ

LESSON 9
(धडा ९ - dhada 9)

हे आईचे स्वयंपाकघर.

This is mother's kitchen.

स्वयंपाकघरात सहा, ताटे बारा वाट्या, सहा भांडी आणि बारा चमचे आहेत.

There are six plates, twelve bowls, six glasses and twelve spoons in the kitchen.

आमच्या कडे दोन पळ्या, दहा डबे, पाच बाटल्या, तीन चिमटे आणि चार पातेली आहेत.

We have two ladles, ten boxes, five bottles, three pincers and four vessels.

आमच्या कडे दोन शेगडया आहेत.

We have two stoves.

Words :

हे = this = he

आईचे = mother = aaiche

सहा = six = saha

ताटे = plates = tate

ताट = a plate = tat

बारा = twelve - bara

वाट्या = bowls - vatya

    ट्या = ट् + य् + आ (ा) = ट्या

वाटी = a bowl = vati

भांडी = glasses = bhandi

भांडं = a glass = bhandn

चमचे = spoons = chamache

चमचा = a spoon = chamacha

पळ्या = ladles = palya

पळी = a ladle = palee

    ळ्या – ळ् + य् + आ (ा) – ळ्या

दहा = ten – daha

डबे = small boxes = dabe

डबा = a small box = daba

पाच = five = pach

बाटल्या = bottles = batalya

    ल्या – ल् + य् + आ (ा) – ल्या

बाटली = a bottle = batalee

तीन = three = teen

चिमटे = pincers = chimate

चिमटा = a pincer = chimata

चार = four = char

पातेली = vessels = pateli

पातेलं = a vessel = pateln (*n* is silent)

आमच्या कडे = we have = amchya kade

च्या = च् + य् + आ (ा) = च्या

शेगड्या = stoves = shegadya

शेगडी = stove = shegadi

इया – इ + य् + आ (ा) = इया

LESSON 10
(धडा 10 - dhada 10)

मी सकाळी पाच वाजता उठतो
I get up in the morning at five o'clock.

नंतर मी अंघोळ करतो
Then I take bath.

मग देवाला नमस्कार करून दूध पितो
After praying to God I drink milk.

मी सळा आठला आभ्यासाला बसतो
I do my home-work at eight-fifteen.

मी साडे नऊ पर्यंत अभ्यास करतो
I do my study until half past nine.

मग आई जेवायला वाढते
Then mother serves the food

जेवायला भात, आमटी, भाजी, पोळी, चटणी, कोशिंबीर, तूप, लोणचे, दही, साखर, दूध असते
We eat cooked rice, curry, vegetable, bread, chutney, koshimbeer, ghee, pickle, curd, sugar and milk at our meal

माझी शाळा दहा वाजता असते
My school starts at ten o'clock.

म्हणून मी पावणे दहाला घराबाहेर पडतो
So I depart from my house at quarter to ten.

वर्गात मी अभ्यास करतो
I do my lessons in the class room.

मी दुपारी तीन वाजता घरी येतो
I come to the home at three o'clock in the afternoon.

मग मी फराळ करतो
Then I take a light repast.

थोड्यावेळ अभ्यास करून संध्याकाळी खेळायला जातो
I study for a while and then go to play in the evening.

रात्री जेवण करून दहा वाजता मी झोपून जातो
I go to bed at ten o'clock after dinner.

LESSON 11
(धडा 11 - **dhada 11**)

ABOUT VILLAGE

हे माझे गाव आहे
This is my village.

गावात दहा पंधरा झोपडया आहेत
There are ten or fifteen huts in the village.

गावात एक ही बंगला नाही
There is no bungalow in the village.

गावात एक विहीर आहे
There is a well in the village.

गावामध्ये एक देऊळ आहे
There is a temple in the village.

गावात काही लोक शेतकरी आहेत
Some people in the village are farmers.

दोन शिंपी आहेत	two are tailors
एक न्हावी आहे	one is barber
एक धोबी आहे	one is washerman
दोन सुतार आहेत	two are carpenters

एक सोनार आहे

आणि एक वाणी आहे

गावात एक ही डॉक्टर नाही

one is goldsmith

and one is grocer

There is no doctor in the village.

गावात कोणी वकील नाही

There is no lawyer in the village.

एक मास्तर शाळा चालवतात

Only one teacher manages the school.

LESSON 12
(धडा 12 – dhada 12)

Dog barks	कुत्रा भुंकतो
Cow lows	गाय हंबरते
Lion roars	सिंह गर्जना करतो
Bullock lows	बैल हंबरतो
Buffalo lows	म्हैस हंबरते
Cat eats mice	मांजर उंदीर खाते
Deer runs	हरण धावते
Monkey jumps	माकड उड्या मारते
Elephant trumpets	हत्ती चीत्कार करतो
Horse neighs	घोडा खिंकाळतो
Donkey eats	गाढव खाते
Goat grazes	शेळी चरते
Male goat has beard	बोकडाला दाढी असते
Sheep gives wool	मेंढी लोकर देते
Tiger roars	वाघ डरकावतो

LESSON 13
(धडा 13 - dhada 13)

Peacock is India's national bird.
मोर भारताचा राष्ट्रीय पक्षी आहे

Cuckoo sings very sweet.
कोकिळा गोड गाते

The crow is black.
कावळा काळा असतो

Sparrow eats grains.
चिमणी दाणे खाते

The beak of the parrot is red.
पोपटाची चोच लाल असते

Swan is a beautiful bird.
हंस सुंदर पक्षी आहे

Pigeons are in two colours, one is white and the other is gray.
कबुतरे दोन रंगाची असतात एक पांढरे व दुसरे राखाडी

Duck swims in the water.
बदक पाण्यात पोहते

बगळा मासे खातो

Owl sits in cavity.
घुबड ढोलीत बसते

The cock crows early in the morning.
कोंबडा सकाळी आरवतो

Hen gives eggs.
कोंबडी अंडी देते

Eagle is the king of birds.
गरूड पक्षांचा राजा आहे

Kite flies high in the sky.
घार आकाशात उंच उडते

Jay perches on a tree.
मैना झाडावर बसली आहे

Pea-hen has no plumage.
लंडोरीला पिसारा नसतो

LESSON 14
(धडा ३ - dhada 3)

Please come here, my house is near.

कृपा करुन येथे ये, माझे घर जवळ आहे.

(krupa karun yethe ye, majhe ghar jawal ahe)

There are three rooms in my house.

माझ्या घरात तीन खोल्या आहेत.

(majhya gharant teen kholiya ahet)

There is one kitchen, one bathroom and one lavatory.

एक स्वयंपाकघर, एक स्नानगृह, आणि एक संडास आहे.

(ek swayampakghar, ek snangrih, ani ek sandas ahe)

There are two beds in each room.

प्रत्येक खोलीत दोन पलंग आहेत.

(pratiek kholit don palang ahet)

The rent of the house is two hundred rupees.

घराचे भाडे दोन शे रुपये आहे.

(gharache bhare don she rupaye ahe)

Our school is near our house.

आमची शाळा आमच्या घरापासून जवळ आहे.

(amchi shala amchiya gharapasoon jawal ahe)

Wait a little, listen to what I say.

जरा थांब, माझे म्हणणे ऐक.

(jara thamb, majhe mahanne aik)

Close the door, go there and send the servant.

दरबाजा बंद करुन, तेथे जा, आणि नोकर पाठव.

(drawaja band karun, tethe, ja, ani nokar pathav)

Open the door and see who is there.

दरवाजा उघड आणि कोण आहे ते पहा.

(darwaja ughad ani kon ahe te paha)

Do this work, help me clean the house.

हे काम कर, मला घर साफ करायला मदत कर.

(hay kam kar, mala ghar saf karayla madat kar)

My mother cooks; though she has become old she works hard.

माझी आई जेवण करते; जरी ती वृद्ध झाली आहे तरी ती खूप काम करते.

(majhi aye jevan karte jari ti wrudhha jhali ahe tari ti khoop kam karte)

I have two brothers and one sister.

मला दोन भाऊ आणि एक बहीण आहे.

(mala don bhau ani ek baheen ahe)

My elder brother is in his room.

माझा मोठा भाऊ त्याच्या खोलीत आहे.

(majha motha bhau tayachya kholeet ahe)

CHAPTER 5
Grammar

LESSON 1
(धडा 10 - dhadam 10)

Verb and Tenses
(क्रियापदे आणि काळ)

In Marathi as in Hindi and Gujarati, the verb comes last and the form of the verb changes in accordance with the gender, person and number of the subject. We will discuss the verb in three tenses.

PRESENT TENSE
वर्तमान काळ (Vartman Kal)

Do कर (kar), look बघ (bagh), run धाव (dhav), go जा (ja), write लिहि (lihi)

I do	मी करते *(feminine)*	मी करतो *(masculine)*
I go	मी जाते *(feminine)*	मी जातो *(masculine)*

I look	मी बघते (*feminine*)	मी बघते (*masculine*)
I run	मी धावते (*feminine*)	मी धावतो (*masculine*)
I write	मी लिहिते (*feminine*)	मी लिहितो (*masculine*)

When the number is changed

We do	आम्ही करतो	(*both masculine & feminine*)
We go	आम्ही जातो	(*both masculine & feminine*)
We look	आम्ही बघतो	(*both masculine & feminine*)
We run	आम्ही धावतो	(*both masculine & feminine*)
We write	आम्ही लिहितो	(*both masculine & feminine*)

When the person is changed

Second person

You do	तू करतोस (*masculine*) *singular*
You do	तू करतेस (*feminine*) *singular*
You do	तुम्ही करता (*masculine & feminine*) *plural*
You go	तू जातोस (*masculine*) *singular*
You go	तू जातेस (*feminine*) *singular*
You go	तुम्ही जाता (*masculine & feminine*) *plural*

Third person

He does	तो करतो (*masculine*)
She does	ती करते (*feminine*)
They do	ते करतात (*masculine*) .
They do	त्या करतात (*feminine*)
He goes	तो जातो (*masculine*)

She goes	ती जाते (*feminine*)
They go	ते जातात (*masculine*)
They go	त्या जातात (*feminine*)

Other Examples

I teach	मी शिकवितो (*m*)	मी शिकविते (*f*)
You teach	तू शिकवितो (*m*)	तू शिकविते (*f*) *singular*
He teaches	तो शिकवितो (*m*)	ती शिकविते (*f*)
I learn	मी शिकतो (*m*)	मी शिकते (*f*)
You learn	तू शिकतो (*m*)	तू शिकते (*f*) *singular*
He learns	तो शिकतो (*m*)	ती शिकते (*f*)
I sit	मी बसतो (*m*)	मी बसते (*f*)
You sit	तू बसतो (*m*)	तू बसते (*f*)
He sits	तो बसतो (*m*)	ती बसते (*f*)

You sit, learn, teach (*masculine, plural*)
तुम्ही (आपण) बसता, शिकता, शिकविता

They sit, learn, teach, (*masculine, plural*)
ते बसतात, शिकतात, शिकवितात

They sit, learn, teach (*feminine, plural*)
त्या बसतात, शिकतात, शिकवितात

It sits ते बसते (*neuter*)
They sit ती बसतात (*neuter*)

Use in Sentences

I write
मी लिहितो
(mi lihito)

I learn Marathi.

मी मराठी शिकतो.

(mi Marathi shikto)

I come here daily.

मी येथे दररोज येतो.

(mi yethe darroj yeto)

I sit on the chair.

मी खुर्चीवर बसतो.

(mi khurchivar basto)

I read a book.

मी पुस्तक वाचतो.

(mi pustak vachto)

We hear a sound.

आम्ही आवाज ऐकतो.

(amhi avaz ekto)

He is here.

तो येथे आहे.

(to yethe ahe)

He is a good man.

तो चांगला मनुष्य आहे.

(to changla manush ahe)

This is good, that is bad.

हे चांगले आहे, ते वाईट आहे.

(he changle ahe, te vayit ahe)

That girl reads a book.

ती मुलगी पुस्तक वाचते.

(tee mulgi pustak vachte)

Cow gives milk.

गाय दूध देते.

(gay dudh dete)

Present Continuous Tense (चालूवर्तमान काळ)

'I am doing', 'we are going', 'she is going', 'he is coming', 'you are doing'– are examples of Present continuous tense.

In such sentences **am, are, is** etc. accompany the subject in the present tense.

I am	मी आहे (mi ahe)	(m. & f.)
we are	आम्ही आहोत (amhi ahot)	(m & f)
she is	ती आहे (ti ahe)	
he is	तो आहे (to ahe)	
they are	ते आहेत (te ahet)	(masculine, plural)
	त्या आहेत (tya ahet)	(feminine, plural)
you are	तू आहेस (to ahes)	(m & f, both singular)
	तुम्ही आहात (tumhi ahat)	(m & f, both plural)

Use in Sentences

I am doing

मी करत आहे

(mi karat ahe)

84

I am reading.
मी वाचत आहे.
(mi vachat ahe)
I am going.
मी जात आहे.
(mi jat ahe)
We are going.
आम्ही जात आहोत.
(amhi jat ahot)
You are going.
तू जात आहेस.
(to jat ahes)   *singular*
You are doing.
तू करत आहेस.
(to karat ahes)   *singular*
You are reading.
तू वाचत आहेस.
(to vachat ahes)   *singular*
You are going.
तुम्ही जात आहात.
(tumhi jat ahat)   *plural*
He is going.
तो जात आहे.
(to jat ahe)
He is coming.
ती येत आहे.
(to yet ahe)
He is reading.
तो वाचत आहे.
(to vachat ahe)

85

She is going.

ती जात आहे.

(tee jat ahe)

It is going.

ते जात आहे.

(te jat ahe)

They are going. (*masculine*)

ते जात आहेत.

(te jat ahet)

They are going. (*feminine*)

त्या जात आहेत

(tya jat ahet)

They are going. (*neuter*)

ती जात आहेत

(ti jat ahet)

He is going out

तो बाहेर जात आहे

(to baher jat ahe)

Exercise

Translate into Marathi :

I. 1. I learn Marathi.
   2. My brother teaches me.
   3. We take tea.
   4. That girl reads a book.
   5. Cow gives milk.
   6. Our school opens.

II. 1. I am teaching Marathi.
2. I am learning Gujarati.
3. He is eating.
4. You are coming.
5. I am reading.
6. They are going for a walk.

Answers :

I. 1. मी मराठी शिकतो.
2. माझा भाऊ मला शिकवितो.
3. आम्ही चहा पितो.
4. ती मुलगी पुस्तक वाचते.
5. गाय दूध देते.
6. आमची शाळा उघडते.

II. 1. मी मराठी शिकवितो आहे.
2. मी गुजराती शिकतो आहे.
3. तो खात आहे.
4. तू येत आहेस.
5. मी वाचत आहे.
6. ते फिरायला जात आहेत.

Present Perfect Tense (पूर्ण वर्तमान काल):

The sign of this tense is **'to have'** (जवळ असणे) as,
for example :

I have	माझ्या जबळ आहे	(majhya javal ahe)
you have	तुझ्या जवळ आहे	(tujhya javal ahe)
he has	त्याच्या जवळ आहे	(tyachya javal ahe)
we have	आमच्या जवळ आहे	(amchya javal ahe)
you have	तुमच्या जवळ आहे	(tumchya javal ahe)
they have	त्यांच्या जवळ आहे	(tianchya javal ahe)
she has	तिच्या जवळ आहे	(tichya javal ahe)
it has	जवळ आहे	(tichya javal ahe)

87

Use in Sentences (*in the sense of possession*)

I have a book.

माझ्या जवळ एक पुस्तक आहे.

(majhiya javal ek pustak ahe)

You have a book.

तुझ्या जवळ एक पुस्तक आहे.

(tujhiya javal ek pustak ahe)

He has a book.

त्याच्या जवळ एक पुस्तक आहे.

(tyachya javal ek pustak ahe)

We have a book.

आमच्या जवळ एक पुस्तक आहे.

(amchya javal ek pustak ahe)

She has a book.

तिच्या जवळ एक पुस्तक आहे.

(tichya javal ek pustak ahe)

They have a book.

त्यांच्या जवळ एक पुस्तक आहे.

(tianchya javal ek pustak ahe)

She has a dog.	तिच्या जवळ एक कुत्रा आहे.
I have money.	माझ्या जवळ पैसे आहेत.
I have two rupees.	माझ्या जवळ दोन रुपये आहेत.
We have two rupees.	आमच्या जवळ दोन रुपये आहेत.

(**Note:** आहे with singular changes into आहेत with plural)

88

I have two sons and one daughter.

मला दोन मुलगे आणि एक मुलगी आहे.

(**Note** : Here we should use '**आहे**' because it agrees with singular '**मुलगी**' being nearest to it.)

He has a horse.

त्याच्या जवळ एक घोडा आहे.

(tyachya javal ek ghora ahe)

Exercise

Translate into Marathi

1. I have much work.
2. We have one rupee.
3. You have two rupees.
4. They have some money.
5. She has many books.

Answers :

1. माझ्या जवळ पुष्कळ काम आहे.
   (majhya javal pushkal kam ahe)

2. आमच्या जवळ एक रुपया आहे.
   (amchya javal ek rupya ahe)

3. तुझ्या जवळ दोन रुपये आहेत.
   (tujhya javal don rupye ahe)

4. त्यांच्या जवळ थोडे पैसे आहेत.
   (tianchya javal thore paise ahet)

5. तिच्या जवळ पुष्कळ पुस्तके आहेत.
   (tichya javal pushkal pustke ahet)

PAST TENSE

भूत काळ (bhoot kal)

So far we have discussed the Present tense. Now we take up the other tense–**Past Tense.**

भूतकाळ means happenings that had occurred in the past. For instance **ran** is the past tense of **run** (धावणे).

Did केले (Kele). looked बघितले (baghitale), ran धावले (dhavle), went गेलो (gelo), wrote लिहिले (lihile)

I did	मी केले *(feminine)*	मी केले *(mas)*
I went	मी गेले *(feminine)*	मी गेले *(mas)*
I looked	मी बघितले *(feminine)*	मी बघितले *(mas)*
I ran	मी धावले *(feminine)*	मी धावलो *(mas)*
I wrote	मी लिहिले *(feminine)*	मी लिहिले *(mas)*

When the number is changed

We did	आम्ही केले *(both masculine & feminine)*
We went	आम्ही गेलो *(both masculine & feminine)*
We looked	आम्ही बघितले *(both masculine & feminine)*
We ran	आम्ही धावलो *(both masculine & feminine)*
We wrote	आम्ही लिहिले *(both masculine & feminine)*

Second person

You did	तू केले *(masculine) singular*
You did	तू केले *(feminine) singular*
You did	तुम्ही केले *(masculine & feminine) plural*
You went	तू गेला *(masculine) singular*
You went	तू गेली *(feminine) singular*
You went	तुम्ही गेला *(masculine & feminine) plural*

90

Third person

English	Marathi	
He did	त्याने केले	*(masculine) singular*
She did	तिने केले	*(feminine) singular*
They did	त्यांनी केले	*(masculine & feminine) plural*
He went	तो गेला	*(masculine) singular*
She went	ती गेली	*(feminine) singular*
They went	ते गेले	*(masculine) plural*
They went	त्या गेल्या	*(feminine) plural*

Other Examples :

I was	मी होतो (mi hoto) *masculine*
	मी होते (mi hoto) *feminine*
we were	आम्ही होतो (amhi hoto)
he was	तो होता (to hoto)
she was	ती होती (tee hoti)
it was	ते होते (te hote)
they were	ते होते (te hote) *masculine*
you were	तू होतास (too hotas) *sing. masculine*
	तुम्ही (आपण) होता (tumhi-apan-hota) *pl.*
	तू होतीस (too hotis) *sing. feminine*
they were	त्या होत्या (tya hotya) *feminine*
	ती होती (tee hoti) *neuter*

Use in Sentences:

Past Continuous Tense (चालू भूतकाळ) :

I was doing.	मी करत होतो *(masculine)*
	मी करत होते *(feminine)*
We were coming.	आम्ही येत होतो
The boy was going.	मुलगा जात होता
He was going.	तो जात होता
She was writing.	ती लिहित होती

They were going.	ते जात होते (*masculine*)
	त्या जात होत्या (*feminine*)
He was running.	तो धावत होता
She was reading.	ती वाचत होती
I was here.	मी येथे होतो
He was there.	तो तेथे होता

Use of did, had :

'Did' is past tense of 'to do' and 'had' is past tense of 'to have'.

Examples :

I went (I did go). मी गेलो.

He came (he did come). तो आला.

I came (did come) back.

मी परत आलो (mi parat alo).

You came back.

तू परत आलास (tu parat alas).

She came back.

ती परत आली (ti parat ali).

We came back.

आम्ही परत आलो (amhi parat alo).

They came back.

ते परत आले (te parat ale).

You came back .

तुम्ही परत आलात (tumhi parat alat).

'आला' is the past tense of येणे (yene) to come.

Similarly, other verbs can be changed.

to go जाणे	गेला went
to say म्हणणे	म्हणाला said
to stay राहणे	राहिला stayed
to run धावगे	धावला ran

to stop थांबणे	थांबला	stopped
to eat जेवणे	जेवला	ate
to speak बोलणे	बोलला	spoke
to give देणे	दिले	gave
to take घेणे	घेतले	took
to do करणे	केले	did
to hear ऐकणे	एकले	heard
to bring आणणे	आणले	brought
to leave सोडणे	सोडले	left
to make बनविणे	बनविले	made
to drink पिणे	प्यायले	drank
to see पाहणे	पाहिले	saw
to send पाठविणे	पाठवविले	sent
to print छापणे	छापलेले	printed

Other Examples :

We went back.	आम्ही परत गेलो.
We asked.	आम्ही विचारले.
He returned.	तो परत आला.
They arrived.	ते येऊन पोहोचले.
He said.	तो म्हणाला.
We saw.	आम्ही पाहिले.
I went to Mumbai.	मी मुंबईला गेलो.
They ran fast.	ते जोराने धावले *(masculine)*.
We opened the door.	आम्ही दरवाजा उघडला.

I gave you one rupee.

मी तुला एक रुपया दिला.

(mitula ek rupaya dila)

I gave him two rupees.

मी त्याला दोन रुपये दिले.

(mi tyala don rupaye dile)

I gave you one chair.

मी तुम्हाला एक खुर्ची दिली.

(mi tumhala ek khurchi dili)

I gave them two chairs.

मी त्यांना दोन खुच्या दिल्या.

(mi tyana don khurchya dilya)

I gave him one book.

मी त्याला एक पुस्तक दिले.

(mi tyala pustak dile)

Rule :

दिला (*singular, masculine*)

दिले (*plural, masculine*)

दिली (*singular, feminine*)

दिल्या (*plural, feminine*)

दिले (*singular, neuter*)

The transitive verb in the past tense must agree with the object in gender and number.

In the above the examples are :

रुपया दिला, रुपये दिले, खुर्ची दिली, खुर्च्या दिल्या

Again if the object is of neuter gender, the form changes into दिले (*singular*) since the **'book'** is neuter gender.

Past Perfect Tense (पूर्ण भूतकाळ) :

Use of 'had'

I had   माझ्या जवळ होते

(*in my possession*)

You had   तुझ्या जवळ होते (*singular*)

तुमच्या (आपल्या) जवळ होते (*plural*)

We had   आमच्या जवळ होते

94

He had	त्याच्या जवळ होते
She had	तिच्या जवळ होते
It had	तिच्या जवळ होते
They had	त्यांच्या जवळ होते

Note : 'होते' (past perfect) is equivalent of आहे (present perfect) meaning **'had'** and **'to have'**

Use in Sentences :

(These sentences do not show anything in possession)

I had gone there.
मी तेथे गेलो होतो.

We had come from school.
आम्ही शाळेतून आलो होतो.

I had gone to school.
मी शाळेत गेलो होतो.

I had given you one rupee.
मी तुम्हाला एक रुपया **दिला होता.**

I had read the book.
मी पुस्तक **वाचले होते.**

I had given them two chairs.
मी त्यांना दोन खूर्च्या **दिल्या होत्या.**

Note : Mark the **black** words. How perfect their endings agree with the objects.

She had met me in Delhi
ती मला दिल्लीला **भेटली होती** (भेटली agrees with होती in feminine gender.)

95

Exercise

I. Translate into Marathi :

1. He came yesterday.
2. He worte one letter.
3. I waited for you.
4. We went to school.
5. I went to your house.
6. They wrote me a letter.
7. I had given him two rupees.

II.
1. I had written him two letters.
2. The train had arrived by 8 o'clock.
3. I bought this book.
4. My brother was in school.
5. A poor man went to a rich man.
6. I had much work yesterday.
7. They were going to bazar.
8. I was going to bazar.
9. The train was running.
10. She was coming for me.
11. I had given him one chair.

96

Answers :

I. 1.   तो काल आला.

    2.   त्याने एक पत्र लिहिले ('त्याने' by him in place of 'तो').

    3.   मी तुमची वाट पाहिली (वाट *feminine*).

    4.   आम्ही शाळेत गेलो.

    5.   मी तुमच्या घरी गेलो.

    6.   त्यांनी मला एक पत्र लिहिले ('त्यांनी' by them).

    7.   मी त्याला दोन रुपये दिले होते.

II. 1.   मी त्याला दोन पत्रे लिहिली होती.

    2.   रेल्वेगाडी आठ वाजता पोहोचली होती.

    3.   मी हे पुस्तक विकत घेतले.

    4.   माझा भाऊ शाळेत होता.

    5.   एक गरीब मनुष्य एका श्रीमंत माणसाकडे गेला.

    6.   काल मला फार काम होते.

    7.   त्या बाजारात जात होत्या.

    8.   मी बाजारात जात होतो.

    9.   गाडी घावत होती.

   10.   ती माझ्याकरता येत होती.

   11.   मी त्याला एक खुर्ची दिली होती.

FUTURE TENSE
भविष्य काळ (bhavishy kal)

To write a sentence in the future tense requires the use of **'will'** or **'shall'** in English. Similarly in Marathi, the words denoting the tense are as follows :

I will do मी करीन (mi katin)

To the root verb '**कर**' is added '**ईन**'

Similarly   I will read=मी वाचीन (mi vachin)

                I shall do=मी करीन (mi karin)

                I shall go=मी जाईन (mi jaeen)

But the ending changes with the person and number. For example :

       we will go = आम्ही जाऊ (amhi jau)

       we shall run = आम्ही धावू (amhi dhau)

       '**ऊ**' is added to the root verb '**जा**' and '**धा**'

       you will go (*singular*) तू जाशील (tu jasheel)

       you will go (*plural*) तुम्ही जाल (tumhi jal)

In these two cases the addition to the root verb 'जा' is made with 'शील' and 'ल'.

he will go	तो जाईल	(to jaeel)
she will go	ती जाईल	(tee jaeel)
it will go	ते जाईल	(te jaeel)

The ending in these cases is 'ईल' but when it comes to plural :

they will go (*masculine*)	ते जातील	(te jateel)
(*feminine*)	त्या जातील	(tya jateel)
(*neuter*)	ती जातील	(tee jateel)
they will sit	ते, त्या, ती बसतील	

Other Examples :

I shall come	मी येईन	(mi yein)
we shall read	आम्ही वाचू	(amhi vanchu)
they will write	ते लिहितील	(te lihiteel)
he will come	तो येईल	(to yaeel)
I shall read	मी वाचीन	(mi vachin)
we will write	आम्ही लिहू	(amhi lihu)

Use in Sentences :

They will return soon.
ते लवकर परत येतील.
(te lavkar parat yeteel)

99

I shall give you the book tomorrow.

मी तुला उद्या पुस्तक देईन.

(mi tula udya pustak deeen)

We shall buy this book.

आम्ही हे पुस्तक विकत घेऊ.

(amhi he pustak vikat gheoo)

He will return soon.

तो लवकर परत येईल.

(to lavkar parat yeeel)

Future Continuous Tense (चालू भविष्यकाळ) :

I shall be	मी असेन (mi asen)	
you will be	तू असशील (too assheel)	*singular*
we shall be	आम्ही असू (amhi asu)	
you will be	तुम्ही असाल (tumhi asal)	*plural*
he will be	तो असेल (to asel)	
she will be	ती असेल (tee asel)	
it will be	ते असेल (te asel)	
they will be	ते असतील (te asteel)	*masculine*
	त्या असतील (tya asteel)	*feminine*
	ती असतील (tee asteel)	*neuter*

Use in Sentences :

I shall be walking.

मी चालत असेन (mi chalat asen)

They will be writing.

ते लिहित असतील *(masculine)*

त्या लिहित असताल *(feminine)*

(te/tya lihit asteel)

We shall be going.

आम्ही जात असू (amhi jat asu)

You will be working.

तुम्ही काम करत असाल

(tumhi kam kart asal)

They will be doing work.

ते काम करत असतील

(te kam karat asteel)

Future Perfect Tense (पूर्ण भविष्यकाळ) :

I shall have come

मी आलो असेन (mi alo asen)

We shall have eaten

आम्ही खाल्ले असेल (amhi khalle asel)

Exercise

Translate into Marathi :

1. I shall think about it.
2. We shall reach there.
3. He will give me the book tomorrow.
4. They will show you my house.

5. I shall not come to school today.
6. I shall go to him at 5 o'clock.
7. He will be eating.
8. He will write a letter.
9. You will be writing.
10. She will be writing.

Answers :

1. मी त्या विषयी विचार करीन.
2. आम्ही तेथे पोहोचू.
3. तो मला उद्या पुस्तक देईल.
4. ते तुम्हाला माझे घर दाखवतील.
5. मी आज शाळेत येत नाही.
6. मी त्याच्या कडे 5 वाजतां जाईन.
7. तो खात असेल.
8. तो पत्र लिहील.
9. तू लिहीत असशील.
10. ती लिहीत असेल.

LESSON 2

(धडा 2 - **dhada 2**)

MORE ABOUT PRONOUNS

We have already given a few pronouns. Here we will discuss some more and in detail.

I मी (mi) ; you तू (tu) *singular*

he तो (to) ; she ती (tee) ;

we आम्ही (amhi) ; you तुम्ही, तू (tumhi, tu) ;

they ते *(masculine)* त्या *(feminine)* ती *(neuter)*

my माझा *(masculine)* ; माझी *(feminine)* ; माझे *(neuter)*

thy तुझा *(masculine)* ; तुझी *(feminine)* ; तुझे *(neuter)*
(in the sense of possession)

his त्याचा *(masculine)* ; त्याची *(feminine)* ; त्यांचे *(neuter)*

her तिचा *(masculine)* ; तिची *(feminine)* ; तिचे *(neuter)*

her तिला

our आमचा *(masculine)* ; आमची *(feminine)* ;
आमचे *(neuter)*

your तुमचा *(masculine)* ; तुमची *(feminine)* ;
तुमचे *(neuter)*

their त्यांचा *(masculine)* ; त्यांची *(feminine)* ;
त्यांचे *(neuter)*

me मला (mala)

him त्याला (tyala)

103

us आम्हाला (amhala)
them त्यांना (tyana)

Use in Sentences :

My book माझे पुस्तक (majhe pustak); **majhe** is used because **book** is neuter gender.

Your son तुमचा मुलगा (tumcha mulga); तुमचा is used because **son** is masculine.

Our clothes आमचे कपडे (amche kapde); आमचे is used because **clothes** is neuter gender.

Similarly the pronoun's form must agree with the gender of the subject.

Other examples :

My horse	माझा घोडा	
My mare	माझा घोडी	
My cap	माझी टोपी	टोपी is *feminine gender*
My chair	माझी खुर्ची	खुर्ची *feminine gender*
My house	माझे घर	घर *neuter gender*
His daughter	त्याची मुलगी	मुलगी *feminine gender*
His book	त्याचे पुस्तक	पुस्तक *neuter gender*
His horse	त्याचा घोडा	घोडा *masculine gender*
His shop	त्याचे दुकान	दुकान *neuter gender*
His address	त्याचा पता	पता *masculine gender*

Her book	तिचे पुस्तक	
Her bag	तिची पिशवी	पिशवी *feminine gender*
Our box	आमची पेटी	पेटी *feminine gender*
Our book	आमचे पुस्तक	
Our work	आमचे काम	काम *neuter gender*
Our office	आमचे आफिस	आफिस *neuter gender*
Your name	तुमचे नांव	नांव *neuter gender*
Your table	तुमचे मेज	मेज *neuter gender*
Your garden	तुमची बाग	बाग *neuter gender*
Your house	तुमचे घर	घर *neuter gender*
Your book	तुझे पुस्तक	
Their book	त्यांवे घर	
Their house	त्यांची घर	
Their toys	त्यांची खेळणी	खेळणी *feminine gender*
Their pay	त्यांचा पगार	पगार *masculine gender*
My son	माझा मुलगा	मुलगा *masculine gender*
My book	माझे पुस्तक	
My horse	माझा घोडा	
Thy cap	तुझी टोपी	

105

LESSON 3

(घडा 3 – dhada 3)

ADJECTIVES

(विशेषणे)

There are two categories of adjectives-which end in **aa** (आ) as चांगला (**good**); मोठा (**big**). Such adjectives change their form in accordance with the gender and number of the nouns they qualify.

For instance :

चांगला मुलगा (good boy)=**boy** is *masculine*

but चांगली मुलगी (good girl)= **girl** is *feminine*

and चांगले घर (good house) = **house** is *neuter*

Similarly in the plural form of the noun the change in the adjective will be as follows :

चांगले मुलगे (good boys)

चांगल्या मुली (good girls)

चांगली घरे (good houses)

The other category of adjectives is made of words which in their masculine form do not end in आ. Such

106

adjectives remain unchanged irrespective of the change in the gender and number of the noun they qualify. For example :

लहान घर (small house)

लहान घरे (small house)

नवें पुस्तक (a new book)

नवी पुस्तके (new books)

सुंदर मुलगा (beautiful boy)

सुंदर मुलगी (beautiful girl)

Other Examples :

good man चांगला मनुष्य;

cheap box स्वस्त पेटी;

bad man वाईट मनुष्य;

cold water थंड पाणी;

cheap grain स्वस्त धान्य;

big room मोठी खोली

Use in Sentences :

This is a good book.

हे एक चांगले पुस्तक आहे.

(hay ek changle pustak ahe)

That is not a bad book.

ते एक वाईट पुस्तक नाही.

(te ek vayit pustak nahin)

That man is rich.

तो मनुष्य श्रीमंत आहे.

(to manushya shrimant ahe)

That is a good man.

तो एक चांगला मनुष्य आहे.

(to ek changla manush ahe)]

This table is dirty.

हे मेज घाणेरडे आहे.

(hay mez ghanerade ahe)

This man is poor.

हा मनुष्य गरीब आहे.

(ha manush garib ahe)

He is a good man.

तो चांगला मनुष्य आहे.

(to changla manush ahe)

This water is cold.

हे पाणी थंड आहे.

(hay pani thand ahe)

That is bad.

ते वाईट आहे.

(te vayit ahe)

This is not bad.

ते वाईट नाही.

(te vayit nahin)

This is good.

हे चांगले आहे.

(he changle ahe)

This is not good.

हे चांगले नाही.

(he changle nahin)

The horse is brown.

घोडा तपकिरी आहे.

(ghora tapkiri ahe)

Ram is clever.

राम हुशार आहे.

(Ram hushar ahe)

Tea is not hot.

चहा गरम नाही.

(chaha garam nahi)

Some adjectives :

छान	nice	chhan
उत्तम	best	uttam
प्रेमळ	loving	premal
दुष्ट	cruel	dusht
गोरा	fair	gora
काळा	black, dark	kala
सरळ	straight	saral
वाकडा	bent, crooked	vakada
घाण	dirt	ghan
सुवासिक	fragrant	suvasik
मोठा	big, elder	motha
छोटा	small, younger	chota
जाड	thick	jad
बारीक	thin	bareek
ताजा	fresh	taja
शिळा	stale	shila
उद्योगी	hard worker industrious	udyogi
आळशी	lazy	alashi
गरम	hot	garam
थंड	cold	thand
आनंदी	happy, joyful	anandi
घाणेरडा	dirty	ghanerda
केसाळ	hairy	kesal

सुंदर	beautiful	sundar
हुशार	intelligent	hushar
लांब	long	laamb
रुंद	broad	rund
प्रामाणिक	konest	pramanik
स्वच्छ	clean	swachha
लोभी	greedy	lobhee
शुद्ध	pure	shudh
पारदर्शक	transparent	pardarshak
पातळ	thin	patal
गोड	sweet	god

Exercise

Translate into Marathi :

1. a tall man
2. great men
3. dirty clothes
4. clever girl
5. short leg
6. honest boy

Answers :

1. एक उंच मनुष्य
2. मोठी माणसे
3. घाणेरडे कपडे
4. हुशार मुलगी
5. बुटके पाय
6. प्रामाणिक मुलगा

LESSON 4
(धडा 4–dhada 4)

MORE ABOUT ADJECTIVES
Degres of Comparison
(तुलनात्मक रुप)

There are *three* degrees of adjectives :

       – **positive** (मूळ विशेषण)
       – **comparative** (अधिकता दर्शक रुप)
       – **superlative** (श्रेष्ठता दर्शक रुप)

मूळ विशेषण हुषार (clever)
अधिकता दर्शक रुप - अधिक हुषार (more clever *or* cleverer)
                          (*comparison between two*)
श्रेष्ठता दर्शक रुप – सर्वात हुषार (cleverest)
                          (*comparison with all*)

Similarly,
brave शूर; braver अधिक शूर; bravest सर्वात शूर

In some cases the superlative form is shown as :
       most learned सर्वात जास्त शिकलेला
       most red सर्वात जास्त लाल

111

Use in Sentences :

This mango is sweet.
हा आंबा गोड आहे.
(ha amba god ahe)

Your watch is slow.
तुमचे घड्याळ मागे आहे.
(tumche ghadyal mange ahe)

Marathi is easier than Gujarati.
मराठी गुजराती पेक्षा सोपी आहे.
(Marathi Gujarati peksha sopi ahe)

This house is smaller than that house.
हे घर त्या घरापेक्षा लहान आहे.
(he ghar tya gharapeksha lahan ahe)

The elephant is the largest animal.
हत्ती सर्व प्राण्यात अतिशय मोठा आहे.
(hatti sarva pranyat atishya motha ahe)

My house is larger than your house.
माझे घर तुझ्या घराहून मोठे आहे.
(majhe ghar tujhya gharahun mothe ahe)

This house is smaller than that house.
हे घर त्या घराहून (घरापेक्षा) लहान आहे.
(he ghar tya gharahun lahan ahe)

This is the smallest house.
हे सर्वात लहान घर आहे.
(he sarvant lahan ghar ahe)

112

This is the largest box.

ही सर्वात मोठी पेटी आहे.

(hi sarvat mothi peti ahe)

This girl is wiser than that boy.

ही मुलगी त्या मुलाहून अधिक शहाणी आहे.

(ha mulgi tya muliuhun adhik shahani ahe)

Exercise

Translate into Marathi :

1. Simla is colder than Delhi.

2. Everest is the highest peak.

3. He is the best teacher.

4. Horse is the fastest animal.

5. He is the weakest man.

Answers :

1. शिमला दिल्लीहून अधिक थंड आहे.

2. एव्हरेस्ट सर्वात अधिक उंच शिखर आहे.

3. तो सर्वात अधिक चांगला शिक्षक आहे.

4. घोडा सर्वात अधिक जलद प्राणी आहे.

    Or

    घोडा सर्व प्राण्यात अधिक (अतिशय) जलद आहे

5. तो सर्वात अधिक दुर्बल माणूस आहे.

113

LESSON 5

(धडा 5-dhada 5)

GENDER
लिंग (ling)

There are *three* genders in Marathi :

1. **Masculine= पुल्लिंग**
2. **Feminine = स्त्रीलिंग**
3. **Neuter= नपुंसक लिंग**

　　मुलगा – boy *(masculine)*

　　मुलगी – girl *(feminine)*

　　मूल – a baby *(neuter)*

ते मेज　　　　　that table *(neuter)*

ती खुर्ची　　　　that chair *(feminine)*

तो दरवाजा　　　that door *(masculine)*

ते दार　　　　　that door *(neuter)*

तो means *masculine*

ती means *feminine*

ते means *neuter*

114

Some Examples :
Masculine words :

पलंग	bed	palang
माळी	gardener	mali
शेतकरी	farmer	shetkari
स्वैपाकी	cook	swaipaki
सूर्य	sun	soorya
डास	mosquito	das
कावळा	crow	kavala

Feminine words :

मुलगी	girl	mulagee
बाई	woman	bai
खिडकी	window	khidakee
पेटी	bag, box	petee

Neuter words :

मूल	baby	mul
घर	house	ghar
झाड	tree	jhad
फळ	fruit	phal
केले	banana	kele

Rule :

In Marathi the gender is determined by the meaning of the words. The words meaning male are masculine and those meaning female are feminine.

Words meaning inanimate objects have their gender as in Sanskrit if they are derived from that language. There are, however, some exceptions too.

(a) Words ending in 'ए' are generally neuter.

(b) Words ending in इ *or* ई are feminine but if the word means male, the gender will be masculine. For example gardener माळी – this is masculine in spite of 'ई' ending because of its meaning. Similarly धोबी (washerman).

Similarly words ending in अ *or* 'आ' can be masculine *or* feminine according to their meaning and derivation.

सूर्य (sun) ending in 'अ' is *masculine* as in Sanskrit
घर (house) ending in 'अ' is *neuter* as in Sanskrit
केळे (banana) ending in 'ए' is *neuter* as in Sanskrit

LESSON 6

(धडा 6 - **dhada 6**)

NUMBER

वचन (**vachan**)

There are *two* numbers in Marathi as in any other language – **singular** (एक वचन) and **plural** (अनेक वचन).

To make plural from singular there are some rules. One of them is to turn all masculine nouns ending in 'आ' into 'ए' for making them plural. For example :

Singular	*Plural*
आंबा (amba-mango)	आंबे (ambe-mangoes)
मुलगा (mulga-boy)	मुलगे (mulge-boys)
राजा (raja-king)	राजे (raje-kings)
बंगला (bangla-house)	बंगले (bangle-houses)
घोडा (ghoda-horse)	घोडे (ghode-horses)
कुत्रा (kutra-dog)	कुत्रे (kutre-dogs)

117

Masculine nouns not ending in 'आ' do not change. They have the same form in both numbers. In other words nouns ending in 'अ' etc. remain unchanged.

For example :

Singular	*Plural*
पाय (pay-leg)	पाय (legs)
मित्र (mitr-friend)	मित्र (friends)
कान (kan-ear)	कान (ears)
हात (hat-hand)	हात (hands)
दिवस (divas-day)	दिवस (days)
माळी (mali-gardener)	अनेक माळी (gardeners)

The second rule is about feminine nouns. Such nouns generally end in 'ई'. They should be changed into 'या' to make them plural.

For example :

Singular	*Plural*
पेटी (peti-box)	पेट्या (petya-boxes)
नदी (nadi-river)	नद्या (nadya-rivers)
गोटी (goti-marble)	गोट्या (gotya-marbles)
काठी (kathi-wood)	काठ्या (kathya-woods)
माशी (mashi-fly)	माश्या (mashya-flies)

The third rule is again about feminine words. If such nouns end in 'अ' the plural thereof is made by changing the ending into 'आ' *or* 'ई'.

For example :

Singular	Plural
म्हैस (mhais-buffalo)	म्हशी (mhashee-buffaloes)
चूक (chook-mistake)	चुका (chuka-mistakes)
मैत्रिण (maitrin-friend)	मैत्रिणी (maitrini-friends)

Feminine nous other than those falling in the above two categories retain the same form in both numbers.

For example :

Singular	Plural
वस्तु (vastu-thing)	वस्तु (things)

Besides masculine and feminine nouns, there are neuter nouns also. In the case of neuter nouns ending in 'अ' or 'ऊ', their number is changed by changing the ending into 'ए'. In the case of neuter nouns ending in 'ए' this change is made by ending the noun with 'ई' in place of 'ए'.

For example :

Singular	Plural
शहर (shahr-city)	शहरे (shahre-cities)
शेत (shet-farm)	शेते (shete-farms)
खोकं (khokan-box)	खोके (khoke-boxes)
गुरे (gure-animal)	गुरे (gure-animals)
केळे (kele-banana)	केळी (keli-bananas)
घड्याळ (ghadyal-watch)	घड्याळे (ghadyal-watches)

Use in Sentences :

मूल = child -- मुले = children

I have two children.

मला दोन मुले आहेत.

खोली=room – खोल्या rooms

I have two rooms.

मला दोन खोल्या आहेत.

There are four rooms in this house.

ह्या घरात चार खोल्या आहेत.

रुपया=rupee – रुपये = rupees

There are ten rupees in this bag.

ह्या पिशवीत दहा रुपये आहेत.

पेटी=box – पेट्या=boxes

I have two boxes.

माझ्यापाशी दोन पेट्या आहेत.

पुस्तक=book – पुस्तके=books

She has many books.

तिच्या जवळ पुष्कळ पुस्तके आहेत.

मित्र=friend – मित्र=friends

There were two friends.

दोन मित्र होते.

Use of number with nouns and pronouns in possessive sense :

The rule is that a singular *or* plural noun is used in accordance with the number of the subject.
For example :

my friend	माझा मित्र
but my friends	माझे मित्र
your box	तुझे खोके
but your boxes	तुझी खोकी
his friend	त्याचा मित्र
but his friends	त्याचे मित्र
his horse	त्याचा घोडा
but his horses	त्याचे घोडे
her friend	तिचा मित्र
but her friends	तिचे मित्र
our friend	आमचा मित्र
but our friends	आमचे मित्र
your book	तुझे पुस्तक
but your books	तुझी पुस्तके
their friend	त्यांचा मित्र
but their friends	त्यांचे मित्र
their book	त्यांचे पुस्तक
but their books	त्यांची पुस्तके

Exercise

Change the numbers :

1. छत्री (umbrella)
2. शेत (farm)
3. माळी (gardener)
4. पेटी (box)
5. घर (house)
6. माणूस (man)
7. स्त्रिया (women)
8. उंदीर (mice)
9. बालके (boys)
10. बैल (ox)

Answers :

1. छत्र्या (umbrellas)
2. शेते (farms)
3. अनेक माळी (gardeners)
4. पेट्या (many boxes)
5. अनेक घरे (many houses)
6. माणसे (men)
7. स्त्री (woman)
8. उंदीर (mouse)
9. बालक (boy)
10. अनेक बैल (oxen)

Note : In the possessive case the system of changing singular into plural is as follows :

boy's book	एक मुलाचे पुस्तक
boys' books	मुलांची पुस्तके
men's houses	लोकांची घरे

In the case of inanimate subjects :

legs of table	टेबलाचे पाय

LESSON 7
(धडा 7 - dhada 7)

CASE ENDINGS
(विभक्ति-प्रत्यय)

This is one of most important chapters without understanding which it is impossible to write correct language. The case determines the change in the ending of the noun. We have already used many a noun in accordance with their cases, but a detailed study is given below:

There are eight cases as in English. We take them up one by one.

1. Nominative Case – प्रथम विभक्ति (कर्ता) :

प्रथमा विभक्तिला प्रत्यय नाही : In this case there are no case-endings. The nominative is used as it is. For example, **I** (मी), **we** (आम्ही) in the first person; **you** (तू), **you** (तुम्ही), plural, in the second person and तो, ती, ते (he, she, it), ते, त्या, ती (they) in the third person remain unchanged.

123

2. Accusative Case--द्विताया विभक्ति (कर्म)

It is also called objective case. Its signs are सा, ला in the singular and ना in the plural nominative. सा, ला and ना are equivalent of 'to' in English.

Use in Sentences :

> **to the house** घराला *or* घरास
> **to this man** ह्या मनुष्याला

I am not going to office today.
मी आज ऑफिसला जात नाही.
(mi aj offisla jat nahi)

This train is going to Poona.
ही आगगाडी पुण्यास जात आहे.
(hi aaggadi puniyas jat ahe)

I am very glad to see you.
तुम्हाला भेटल्या मुळे मला फार आनंद झाला आहे.
(tumhala bhetliya mule mala far anand jhala ahe)

3. Instrumental Case – तृतीया विभक्ति

The signs of the case-ending are **by** (ने) and **with** (शी) in the singular and **by** (नो), **with** (शी) in the plural. It is **by me** (मी), **by us** (आम्ही) in the first person, **by you** (तूं), **by you** (तुम्ही *plural*) in the second person and **by him** (त्याने), **by her** (तिने), **by that**

(त्याने) in singular and **by them** (त्यांनी) in plural in third person.

Use in Sentences :

He should go **by** this road.

त्याने ह्या रस्त्याने जावे.

(tyane hya rastyane jave)

He killed the enemy **with** his sword.

त्याने तलवारीने शत्रुला ठार केले (मारले).

(tyane talwarine shatrula thar kele (marle)

She killed a dog **with** her gun.

तिने बंदुकीने एक कुत्रा मारला.

(tine bandookine ek kutra marla)

He killed a fly (A fly was killed by him).

त्याने माशी मारली.

(tyane mashi marli)

He went by train.

तो आगगाडीने गेला.

(to aggadine gela)

I cut a mango with a knife.

मी सुरीने आंबा कापतो

mi surine amba kapto)

4. Dative Case–चतुर्थी विभक्ति (संप्रदान)

The case-endings of the nominative in this case are **for** (स, ला) in singular and ना in plural. Examples :

for me (मला); for us (आम्हाला); for you (तुला); for
you, *plural* (तुम्हाला); for him (त्याला); for her (तिला);
for it (त्याला); for them (त्यांना).

Use in Sentences :

We went **for** a picnic.
आम्ही पिकनिकला गेलो.
(amhi picnikla gelo)

They are going **for** a walk.
ते फिरायला जात आहेत.
(te firayla jat ahet)

How much **for** this?
याची किती किंमत ?
(yachi kiti kimmat)

5. Ablative Case–पंचमी (अपादान)

The endings in this case are **from** (पासुन), **than**
(पाहून) *or* (ऊन) in singular and the same in plural of
nominatives. **from=**पासून; **than=**पाहून

Use in Sentences :

From this office	from the office
ह्या ऑफिस पासून	ऑफिस पासून
(hya office pasun)	
From the house	घरापासून; घराहून

126

My brother comes from the school.

माझा भाऊ शाळेतून येतो.

Mail goes from here on Saturday.

येथून शनिवारी मेल जाते.

I have come from Mumbai.

मी मुंबईहून आलो आहे.

This boy is wiser than that boy.

हा मुलगा त्या मुलाहून अधिक शहाणा आहे.

6. **Possessive Case** – षष्ठी विभक्ति (संबंध)

The case-endings are **of** (चा, ची, चे) in singular and चे, च्या, ची in plural.

Use in Sentences :

of the man – मनुष्याचा
of the woman – स्त्रीची
of your brother – तुमच्या भावाचे
of the book – पुस्तकाचे

The water of the river is good.

नदीचे पाणी चांगले आहे.

(nadiche pani changle ahe)

What is the price of this?

ह्याची किमत काय ?

(hyachi keenmat kaye)

Sons of Adam and Eve.

आदम व ईव्हचे मुलगे.

(Adam va Eveche mulge)

127

Brother's share
भावाचा वाटा
(bhavachha wata)

Who is the owner of this house?
या (ह्या) घराचा मालक कोण आहे ?
(ya (hya) gharacha malak kon ahe)

What is the good of that?
त्याचा काय फायदा आहे
(tyacha kae fayda ahe)

The page of the book
पुस्तकाचे पान
(pustkache pan)

It is an hour's journey.
एक तासाचा रस्ता आहे
(ek tasacha rasta ahe)

Two hours' walk
दोन तासांची सहल आहे
(don tasanchi sahal ahe)

Father's name
बापाचे नाव,   वडिलांचे नाव
(bapache nav)   (vadilanche nav)

The back side of their house
त्यांच्या घराची मागची बाजू
(tyanchya gharachi magchi baju)

128

What is the rent of the house?

घराचे भाडे किती ?

(gharache bhade kiti?)

This man is his brother.

हा मनुष्य त्याचा भाऊ आहे.

(ha manush tyacha bhau ahe)

What sort of

कोणत्या प्रकारचे

(kontya prakarche)

7. Locative Case – सप्तमी :

The case-endings are **in** (त, ई), **on** (वर) in both singular and plural.

Use in Sentences :

in this house	ह्या घरात	hya gharat
in that box	त्या पेटीत	tya petit
in the morning	सकाळी	sakali
in the evening	संध्याकाळी	sandhyakali
in our hour	एका तासात	eka tasat
in five minutes	पाच मिनिटात	pach minitat
in the night	रात्री	ratrin
in this month	ह्या महिन्यात	hya mahinyat
on the table	मेजावर	mejavar
on the horse	घोड्यावर	ghodyavar
on the road	रस्त्यावर	rastyavar

129

There are ten rupees in the bag.

पिशवीत दहा रुपये आहेत.

(pishavit daha rupay ahet)

There is no sugar in the tea.

चहात साखर नाही (chahat sakhar nahi)

I stayed in the hotel.

मी होटेलात राहिलो.

(mi hotelat rahilo)

My coat was in the box.

माझा कोट पेटीत होता.

maza kot petit hota)

I was in school yesterday.

मी काल शाळेत होतो.

(mi kal shalet hoto)

We live in the city.

आम्ही शहरांत रहातो.

(amhi shahrat rahato)

Who lives in that house?

त्या घरात कोण रहातो ?

(tya gharat kon rahato)

The book was on the table.

पुस्तक मेजावर होते.

(pustak mejavar hote)

Put water in the bottle.

बॉटलीत पाणी घाल.

(batlit pani ghal)

Put this letter on my table.

हे पत्र माझ्या टेबलावर ठेव.

(he patr majhya tebleavar thev)

My father is at Belgaum.

माझे वडील बेळगावात आहेत.

(Majhe vadil belgavat ahet)

8. **Vocative Case—संबोधन :**

This case expresses the person addressed to.

Ah! this man is poor.

अरे ! हा माणूस गरीब आहे

(aray! ha manus garib ahe)

Oh friend!

अरे मित्रा !

(aray mitra)

Well, done is done!

बरे, झाले ते झाले !

(bare, jhale te jhale)

Exercise

Translate into Marathi :

1. I live in this house.
2. There are four room in this house.
3. Put these things in the carriage.
4. Put it in that box.

131

5. We play tennis in the evening.
6. My brother works in this office.
7. She stayed in this house.
8. I have pain in the stomach.
9. Send this book to Gobind.
10. Take this parcel to my house.
11. With this man.
12. Come with me.
13. I discussed with Ram.
14. Put that on the table.
15. Is your school very far from here?
16. Mail goes from here on Saturday.
17. Mohan has taken your book from me.
18. I have worked for four hours.
19. One month's leave.
20. Boy's, boys', of the man.

Answers :

1. मी ह्या घरात राहतो.
2. ह्या घरात चार खोल्या आहेत.
3. ह्या वस्तु गाडीत ठेव.
4. ते पेटीत ठेव.
5. आम्ही संध्याकाळी टेनिस खेळतो.
6. माझा भाऊ ह्या ऑफिसांत काम करितो.
7. ती ह्या घरात राहिली.
8. माझ्या पोटात दुखत आहे.

9. हे पुस्तक गोविन्दाकडे पाठवून दे.

10. हे पार्सल माझ्या घरी घेऊन जा.

11. ह्या मनुष्या बरोबर.

12. माझ्या बरोबर ये.

13. मी रामबरोबर चर्चा केली.

14. ते मेजावर ठेव.

15. तुझी शाळा येथून फार दूर आहे काय ?

16. येथून शनिवारी मेल जाते.

17. मोहनने तुमचे पुस्तक माझ्यापासून घेतले आहे.

18. मी चार तास काम केले आहे.

19. एक महिन्याची रजा.

20. मुलाचा, मुलांचे, मनुष्याचा.

LESSON 8
(धडा ८ - dhada 8)

MISCELLANEOUS EXPRESSIONS

Use of *No* (नाहीं नकोस)

So far we have discussed the affirmative sentences. We will now discuss the negative sentences. For example :

I am not going.
मी जात नाही. (Mi jat nahi)

I am not going to office today.
मी आज ऑफिसला जात नाही.
(mi aj afisla jat nahi)

He is not at home.
ते घरी नाहीत.

They have no money.
त्यांच्या जवळ पैसे नाहीत.

From the above examples, it is clear that the negative **no** (नाही) comes at the end of the sentence in Marathi and is changed in accordance with the subject it is related to.

No means नाही and Don't means मत करू नकोस.

मी – नाही
ते – नाहीत
त्यांच्या – नाहीत

But in sentences like the following नाहीं is **not** used at the end.

No, the bank is open today.
नाही, बँक आज उघडी आहे.
(nahi bank aj ughdi ahe)

No, he is a carpenter.
नाही, तो सुतार आहे.
(nahi, to sutar ahe)

Other Examples :

I have no time.
मला वेळ नाही.
(mala vel nahi)

There is no sugar in tea.
चहात साखर नाही
(chahat sakhar nahin)

This milk is good.
हे दूध चांगले नाही.
(he dudh changle nahi)

No, it (house) is near.
नाही, ते घर जवळ आहे.
(nahi, te ghar jawal ahe)

He is not going out.
तो बाहेर जात नाही.
(to baher jat nahi)

I shall not go.
मी जाणार नाही.
(mi janar nahi)

He does not come here.
तो येथे येत नाही.
(to yethe yet nahi)

I did not go.
मी गेलो नाही.
(mi gelo nahi)

We did not go.
आम्ही गेलो नाही.
(amhi gelo nahi)

You did not go.
तू गेला नाहीस *Or* तुम्ही गेला नाही.
(tu gela nahis *Or* tumhi gela nahi)

He did not go.
तो गेला नाही.
(to gela nahi)

They did not go.
ते गेले नाहीत.
(te gele nahit)

136

Use of Don't (नकोस) :

Don't come.

येऊ नकोस.

(yeoo nakos)

Don't take.

घेऊ नकोस.

(gheoo nakos)

Don't make a noise.

आवाज करु नकोस.

(awaj karoo nakos)

Don't fight.

लढाई करु नकोस.

(ladhai karu nakos)

Exercise

I. Translate into Marathi :

1. They have no money.
2. I have no money.
3. No, there is no shop in the city.
4. No, the dinner is not ready yet.
5. Don't take any food.
6. I am not quite well.
7. I am not sure.
8. He did not come here.

9. Don't put so much milk in tea.
10. Don't go without me.
11. Don't forget.
12. Don't ask me.
13. This is not bad.

Answers :

1. त्यांच्या जवळ पैसे नाहीत.
2. माझ्या जवळ पैसे नाहीत.
3. नाही, शहरात दुसरे दुकान नाही.
4. नाही, जेवण अजून तयार झाले नाही.
5. कोणतेही अन्न घेऊ नकोस.
6. मी अगदी बरा नाही.
7. मला खात्री नाही.
8. तो येथे आला नाही.
9. इतके दूध चहात घालू नकोस.
10. माझ्या शिवाय जाऊ नकोस.
11. विसरु नकोस.
12. मला विचारु नकोस.
13. ते वाईट नाही.

LESSON 9
(धडा 9 - dhada 9)

AFFIRMATIVES–NEGATIVES

Affirmatives	*Negatives*
He goes – तो जातो	He does not go – तो जात नाही
You go – तू जा	Don't go – तू जाऊ नकोस
I go – मी जातो	I don't go – मी जात नाही
Or	
तुम्ही जाता	
We go – आम्ही जातो	We do not go – आम्ही जात नाही.
They go – ते जातात	they do not go – ते जात नाही
I shall go – मी जाईन	I shall not go – मी जाणार नाही
He will come – तो येईल	he will not come –तो येणार नाही
I know his name	I do not know his name
मला त्याचे नाव माहीत आहे	मला त्याचे नाव माहीत नाही
He went – तो गेला	he did not go – तो गेला नाही
I went – मी गेलो	I did not go – मी गेलो नाही
We went – आम्ही गेलो	We did not go – आम्ही गेलो नाही
You went – तू गेला	You did not go तू गेला नाही
	Or तुम्ही गेला नाही

139

LESSON 10

(धडा 10 - dhada 10)

THE POTENTIAL MOOD

शकणे (shakane) (to be able)

In this lesson we shall teach the use of **'can'**, **'cannot'** and **'may'**.

I *can* do.

मी करु शकतो.

(mi karoon shakto)

Or

मला करता येते.

(mala karta yete)

I *cannot* do.

मी करु शकत नाही.

(mi karu shakat nahi)

Or

मला देता येते.

(mala deta yete)

I *cannot* give.

मी देऊ शकत नाही.

(mi deoo shakat nahi)

140

I *can* go there.

मी तेथे जाऊ शकतो.

(mi tethe jaoo shakato)

I *cannot* go there.

मी तेथे जाऊ शकत नाही.

(mi tethe jao shakat nahi)

Can you speak Marathi?

तू मराठी बोलू शकतोस काय ?

(tu Marathi bolu shaktos kay?)

I *cannot* speak Marathi.

मी मराठी बोलू शकत नाही.

(mi Marathi boloo shakat nahi)

I *can* speak Marathi.

मला मराठी बोलता येते.

(mala Marathi bolta yetei)

I *cannot* understand Marathi.

मी मराठी समजू शकत नाही.

(mi Marathi samju shakat nahi)

I *could not* understand Marathi.

मी मराठी समजू शकलो नाही.

(mi Marathi samju shaklo nahi)

I *could not* come.

मी येऊ शकलो नाही.

(mi yeoo shaklo nahi)

They *could not* come.
ते येऊ शकलो नाहीत.
(te yeoo shaklo nahit)

Can you write Marathi?
तुम्हाला मराठी लिहिता येते काय ?
(tumhala Marathi lihita yete kay)

Use of 'may' :

May I come?
मी येऊ का ?
(mi yeoo ka)

May I go?
मी जाऊ का ?
(mi jaoo ka)

May I call him?
मी त्याला बोलाऊ का ?
(mi tyala bolaoo ka)

May I read this book?
मी हे पुस्तक वाचूं का ?
(mi he pustak vachu ka)

Exercise

Translate into Marathi :

1.	I can bring.	2.	I can read.
3.	We can do.	4.	We can hear.
5.	I can work.	6.	He can write.
7.	They can read.	8.	They could not see.

9. He could not come. 10. Can you read?

11. I can see. 12. Can you tell his name?

13. May I come tomorrow?

Answers :

1. मी आणू शकतो
2. मी वाचू शकतो
3. आम्ही करु शकतो
4. आम्ही ऐकू शकतो
5. मी करु शकता
6. तो लिहू शकतो
7. ते वाचू शकतात
8. ते पाहू शकले नाहीत
9. तो येऊ शकला नाही
10. तुम्ही वाचू शकता काय ?
11. मी पाहू शकतो
12. तुम्ही त्यांचे नाव सांगू शकता काय ?
13. मी उद्या येऊ का ?

Note : The root '**शकणे**' undergoes change with the change in the subject.

LESSON 11

(धडा 11 - dhada 11)

INTERROGATIVES

(प्रश्नर्थक वाक्ये)

'Is' and 'Are' :

Is any one there?

तिकडे कोणी आहे काय ?

Is this my book?

हे पुस्तक माझे आहे काय ?

Are your clothes ready?

तुझे कपडे तयार आहेत काय ?

Are my clothes ready?

माझे कपडे तयार आहेत काय ?

Are you owner of this house?

तुम्ही ह्या घराचे मालक आहात काय ?

Is this letter for me?

हे पत्र माझा करिता आहे काय ?

Is tea ready?

चहा तयार आहे काय ?

Is your house far from here?

तुझे घर येथून लांब आहे काय ?

144

Are you in his service?
आपण त्याच्या नोकरीत आहात ?

Are you at leisure?
तुम्हाला वेळ आहे काय ?

Are you married?
तुझे लग्न झाले आहे काय ?

Are you coming?
तू येत आहेस काय ?

Is that boy your brother?
तो मुलगा तुझा भाऊ आहे का ?

Is this book yours?
हे पुस्तक तुझे आहे का ?

Is this a good book?
हे चांगले पुस्तक आहे का ?

Is he learning Marathi?
तो मराठी शिकत आहे का ?

Is your brother at home?
तुझा बंधू घरी आहे काय ?

Is this their house?
हे घर त्यांचे आहे काय ?

Note : In such sentences **Is** (काय) is used at the
end of the sentence.

What (काय, किती) & Who (कोण, जो)

What is this?	हे काय आहे ?
What is that?	ते काय आहे ?
What is your name?	तुझे नाव काय आहे ?
What is your father's name?	तुझ्या वडिलांचे नाव काय आहे ?
What is your father?	आपले वडील काय करतात ?
What is his name?	त्याचे नाव काय आहे ?
What is the name of this town?	त्या शहराचे नाव काय आहे ?
What sort of fruit is this?	हें फळ कोणत्या प्रकारचे आहे ?
What is the date today?	आज कोणती तारीख आहे ?
	OR आज किती तारीख आहे ?
What is the price of this?	याची किंमत काय आहे ?
What is your age?	तुझे वय किती आहे ?
What is your pay?	तुझा पगार काय आहे ?
What is your advice?	तुझा सल्ला काय आहे ?
What colour is this?	हा रंग कोणता आहे ?
What is the time?	किती वाजले आहेत ?
What is the time now?	आता किती वाजले आहेत ?
What is your address?	तुझा पत्ता काय आहे ?
What is the matter?	काय झाले ? *OR* काय गडबड आहे ?
What are you doing?	तू काय करित (करीत) आहेस ?
What pay you will take?	तू काय (किती) पगार घेशील ?

What did he do?	त्याने काय केले ?
What did you say?	तू काय म्हणालास ?
What did he say?	तो काय म्हणाला ?
(at) What time did you come?	तुम्ही किती वाजता आलात ?
What is the matter with him?	त्याला काय होत आहे ?
What is this thing?	ही वस्तु कसली ?
What will you eat?	तुम्ही काय खाल ?
What will you drink?	तुम्ही काय प्याल ?
What should be done?	काय केले पाहिजे ?
What are you doing?	तू काय करीत आहेस ?
What have you to do with it?	तुम्हास त्या बाबतीत काय घेणे आहे ?

Note : Generally **what** (किती) is used where numbers are meant. 'काय' is used not at the end in sentences beginning with **'what'**.

Who is that man?	तो मनुष्य कोण आहे ?
	OR तो कोण मनुष्य आहे ?
Who is there?	तेथे कोण आहे ?
Who is the owner of this house?	या (ह्या) घराचा मालक कोण आहे ?
Who is he?	तो कोण आहे ?
Who are they?	ते कोण आहेत ?
Who is that boy?	तो मुलगा कोण आहे ?

147

Who are you?	तुम्ही कोण आहात ?
Who was there?	तेथे कोण होता ?
Who will be there?	तेथे कोण असेल ?

Use of How (कस), How large (किती मोठे), How much (किती), How many (किती), How far (किती लांब) :

How do you know that?	तुम्हास ते कसे माहीत झाले ?
How are you?	तुम्ही कसे आहात ? *(plural)*
	तू कसा आहेस ? *(singular)*
How do you do?	कसे काय आहे ?
How is the market today?	आज बाजार कसा आहे ?
How was the market today?	आज बाजार कसा होता ?
How many boys are in the class?	वर्गांत किती मुलगे आहेत ?
How large is that room?	ती खोली किती मोठी आहे ?
How many rooms are there?	किती खोल्या आहेत ?
How many children have you?	तुला किती मुले आहेत ?
How far is your house?	तुमचे घर किती लांब आहे ?
How much for a pound?	एका रत्तलास काय पडेल ?
How much money you have?	तुझ्या जवळ किती पैसे आहेत ?
How mauch sugar is there?	साखर किती आहे ?

Rule : '**किती**' is used for adjectives of the number and measurement. It remains unchanged irrespective of the change in the number of the noun it qualifies in the present tense.

Use of 'where' (कोठे) :

Where is Sita?	सीता कुठे (कोठे) आहे ?
Where is Ram?	काम कोठे आहे ?
Where is he?	तो कोठे आहे ?
Where is your office?	तुझे ऑफिस कोठे आहे ?
Where is his office?	त्याचे ऑफिस कोठे आहे ?
Where are the students?	विद्यार्थी कोठे आहेत ?
Where are you going?	तू कोठे जात आहेस ?
Where are you employed?	तुला नोकरी कोठे आहे ?
Where were you yesterday?	तू काल कोठे होतास ?
	OR काल तू कोठे होतास ?
Where was he yesterday?	काल तो कोठे होता ?
Where were they yesterday?	ते काल कोठे होते ?
Where does he live?	तो कोठे राहतो ?
Where do you work?	तुम्ही कोठे काम करतां ?
Where did you live?	तू कोठे राहतोस ?
Where did he go?	तो कोठे गेला
Where did she go?	ती कोठे गेली ?
Where did you go?	तुम्ही कोठे गेला होता ?

Where has he gone?	तो कोठे गेला आहे ?
Where will you go from here?	येथून आपण कोठे जाणार ?
Where can I get?	मला कोठून मिळू शकेल ?

Use of 'whose' (कोणाचा) :

Whose shop is this?	हे दुकान कोणाचे आहे ?
Whose book is this?	हे कोणाचे पुस्तक आहे ?
Whose son is he?	तो कोणाचा मुलगा आहे ?
Whose box is that?	ती पेटी कोणाची आहे ?

Note : The root कोणाचा undergoes change with gender and number of the subject.

Use of 'which' (कोणते) :

(This is neuter form of 'who')

| which is | कोणते आहे |

Which is the shortest road?
सर्वांत जवळचा रस्ता कोणता ?

Which is the cheapest shop
सर्वांत स्वस्त दुकान कोणते ?

Which is your book?
तुमचे कोणते पुस्तक आहे ?

Use of 'did' :
(past tense of 'do' केले, करणे)

Did is the auxiliary word, as, for instance, did you go there?

Did you go there?	तू तेथे गेलास काय
	or तुम्ही गेलात काय ?
Did I go?	मी गेलो काय ?
Did we go?	आम्ही गेलो काय ?
Did he go?	तो गेला काय ?
Did they go?	तो गेला काय ?
Where did he go?	तो कोठे गेला ?
Why did you go?	तू का गेलास ?
Why did you not go there?	तू तेथे का गेला नाहीस ?
Where did she go?	ती कोठे गेली ?
Where did you go?	तू कोठे गेला होतास ?
What did he say?	तो काय म्हणाला ?
When did he come?	तू काय म्हणालास ?
What did I tell you?	मी तुम्हाला काय म्हणालो (सांगितले)
Did you bring an answer?	तुम्ही उत्तर आणल काय ?
Did you take tea?	तुम्ही चहा प्यालात काय ?
Did you find my house?	तुम्हास माझे घर सापडले का ?

151

Use of 'when' (केव्हां, जेव्हां) and 'why' (कां):

When I began to eat   जेव्हा मी खाऊ लागलो

When does the show begin?   शो केव्हा सुरु होतो ?

When I saw him?   जेव्हा मी त्याला पाहिले

Exercise

Translate into Marathi :

1. Is he a good man?
2. Is it a good book?
3. Is this your seat?
4. Are there any letters for me?
5. Is there anyone here?
6. What is your age?
7. What is your occupation?
8. What is your surname?
9. What do you want?
10. What did I tell you?
11. What else?
12. What station is this?
13. Who lives in that house?
14. How are you now?
15. How large is that room?
16. How many books you have?

17. How much money do you want?
18. How much milk is there?
19. Where is your shop?
20. Where is his horse?
21. Whose house is this?
22. Whose coat is this?
23. Did you do my work?
24. Did you understand?
25. Did you do this in his presence?

Answers :

1. तो चांगला मनुष्य आहे का ?
2. ते चांगले पुस्तक आहे काय ?
3. ही आपली जागा आहे काय ?
4. माझ्याकरिता एकादे पत्र आहे काय ?
5. इकडे कोणी आहे काय ?
6. तुझे वय काय आहे ?
7. तुझा धंदा कोणता ?
8. तुझे आडनाव काय ?
9. तुला काय पाहिजे ?
10. मी तुम्हाला काय म्हणालो ?
11. आणखी काय ?
12. हे स्टेशन कोणते ?
13. त्या घरात कोण रहातो ?
14. तू आता कसा आहेस ?
15. ती खोली किती मोठी आहे ?

16. तुमच्या जवळ किती पुस्तके आहेत ?

17. तुम्हाला किती पैसे पाहिजेत ?

18. दूध किती आहे ?

19. तुझे दुकान कोठे आहे ?

20. त्याचे घर कोठे आहे ?

21. हे घर कोणाचे आहे ?

22. हा कोट कोणाचा आहे ?

23. तुम्ही माझे काम केले काय ?

24. समजले का ?

25. तुम्ही तो हजर असताना हे केले का ?

LESSON 12

(धडा 12 – dhada 12)

IMPERATIVES

Ask me मला विचार; **ask** him त्याला विचार; ask them त्यांना विचार

Be quiet गप्प रहा; be careful सावध रहा; be quick लवकर कर

Bring an answer उत्तर आण; bring tea चहा आण

Call him त्याला बोलाव; call them त्यांना बोलाव; call them here त्यांना येथे **बोलाव**

Come here इकडे ये; come soon लवकर ये; come in time वेळेवर या; come to me मज जवळ ये; come with him त्याच्या बरोबर ये

Do this हे कर; do that ते कर

Go there तेथे जा; go soon लवकर जा; go up वर जा; go down खाली जा; go slowly हळू जा; go straight सरळ जा; go at once ताबडतोब जा

Get down खाली उतरा

Give me मला दे; give us आम्हाला दे

155

Look here इकडे पहा

Make haste लवकर कर

Put on the table टेबलावर ठेव

Sit here येथे बस; sit there तेथे बस

Speak louder मोठ्याने बोला; speak slowly सावकाश बोल; speak clearly स्पष्ट बोल

Take away घेऊन जा

Wait here येथे थांब; wait there तेथे थांब.

CHAPTER 6
CONVERSATION

LESSION 1
(धडा 1 - **dhada 1**)

ABOUT THE WATCH
(वेळ-घडयाळ)

What is the time now?
आता किती वाजले आहेत ?

It is four o'clock.
चार वाजले आहेत

What was the time fifteen minutes ago?
पंधरा मिनिटांपूर्वी किती वाजले होते ?

It wat 15 minutes to four.
चार वाजायला पंधरा मिनिटे होती

It is fifteen minutes past four now.

आता चार वाजून पंधरा मिनिटे झाली आहेत

Or

आता सव्वा चार वाजले आहेत

It is half past four. साडे चार वाजले आहेत

It is half past one. दीड वाजला आहे

It is half past two. अडीच वाजले आहेत

It is 15 minutes to four.

चार वाजायला पंधरा मिनिटे आहेत

At one o'clock एक वाजता

At two o'clock दोन वाजता

It is forty minutes past four now.

आता चार वाजून चाळीस मिनिटे झाली आहेत

I am running in five minutes.

मी पाच मिनिटात धावत आहे

He was running five minutes ago:

तो पाच मिनिटांपूर्वी धावत होता

They were going to bazar an hour ago.

त्या एका तासापूर्वी बाजारात जात होत्या

You were playing cricket at one o'clock.

तुम्ही एक वाजता क्रिकेट खेळत होता

I was going home at half past two.

मी अडीच वाजता घरी जात होते

Will you wait for me at 12-45?

आपण पाउण वाजता माझी वाट पहाणार का ?

It is five minutes to nine.

नऊला पाच मिनिट कमी आहेत

LESSON 2
(धडा 2 – dhada 2)

WITH FRIEND
(मित्राशी)

Sham : Ram, where are you going?
राम, तुम्ही कुठे जाता ?
(Ram, tumhi kuthe jata)

Ram : I am going to school.
मी शाळेला जात आहे.
(mee shalela jaat aahe)

Sham : Stop, listen to what I say.
थांब, माझे म्हणणे ऐक.
(thamb, majhe mhane ek)

Ram : No. I will go, what do you want?
नाही. मी जाईन, तुला काय पाहिजे ?
(nahi. mee jayen, tula kay pahije)

Sham : Let us go to a cinema. The picture is beautiful.
I am sure we will have a jolly good time.
आपण सिनेमाला जाऊ या. हे चित्र सुंदर आहे. मला खात्री आहे
की आपला दिवेळ अगदी मजेत जाईल.

(apan cinemala jao ya. he chitr sunder ahe.
mala khatri ahe ki aple divas agdi majet jateel)

159

Ram : I have seen that picture.
मी ते चित्र पाहिले आहे.
(mee te chitr pahile ahe)

Sham : Wait a little, what is the time?
जरा थांब, किती वाजले ?
(jara thamb, kiti wajle)

Ram : No. I must go.
नाही. मला गेलेच पाहिजे.
(nahi. mala galech pahije)

LESSON 3
(धडा 3 – dhada 3)

What is your name?
तुझे नाव काय ?

My name is Ram.
माझे नाव राम आहे.

How many brothers have you?
तुला किती भाऊ आहेत ?

I have one brother.
मला एक भाऊ आहे.

How many sisters have you?
तुला किती बहिणी आहेत ?

I have one sister.
मला एक बहीण आहे.

What is your brother?
तुझा भाऊ काय करतो ?

He studies in college.
तो महाविद्यालयात शिकतो.

In which year he is studying?
कोणत्या वर्षाला आहे ?

161

He is in fourth year.
तो चौथ्या वर्षाला करते ?

What is your sister?
तुझे बहीण काय शिकते

She also studies in college.
ती पण महाविद्यालयात शिकते

In which year she is stuyding?
कोणत्या वर्षाला आहे

She is in first year.
ती पहिल्या वर्षाला आहे

How are her teachers?
तिचे प्राध्यापक कसे आहेत ?

They are good.
ते चांगले आहेत

When are his exams?
त्याची परीक्षा कधी आहे

His exams are a day after.
त्याची परीक्षा परवा आहे

When do you have holidays?
तुम्हाला सुट्टी कधी आहे ?

We have holidays after a month.
आम्हाला सुट्टी एक महिन्यानी आहे

162

CHAPTER 7
Letter Writing
(पत्र लेखन)

Asking for return of book :

Dear Ram,

Please return my book which I gave you yesterday. I want it for my studies.

Yours sincerely,
Mahindar

प्रिय राम,

कृपा करुन मी तुला काल दिलेले माझे पुस्तक परत पाठव. ते मला अभ्यासाला हवे आहे.

आपला विश्वासू,
महेन्द्र

163

Reply :

Dear Mahindar,

I got your letter this morning. I am sending the book per bearer. Please return it as per your convenience.

Yours sincerely,
Ram

प्रिय, महेन्द्र,

मला तुझे पत्र आज सकाळी पोहोचले. मी पुस्तक पाठवीत आहे. सवडीनुसार परत करावे अशी विनंती आहे.

आपला विश्वासू,
राम

Application for Sick-leave
आजार पणाच्या सुटीचा अर्ज

Head Master,
Sir,

I beg to inform you that I am running fever since yesterday night. I cannot even walk due to fever. Hence I cannot attend school. Kindly grant me leave from 11.10.04 to 13.10.04.

Thanking you,

Your obedient student
Gireesh

मुख्याध्यापक,
गुरुजी,

सविनय निवेदन करत आहे की काल रात्री पासून मला ताप येत आहे. तापामुळे मी चालू पण शकत नाही. त्यामुळे मी शाळेत येऊ शकत नाही. म्हणून कृपया मला दिनांक 11.10.04 ते 13.10.04 पर्यन्त सुटी द्यावी.

धन्यवाद,

आपला आज्ञाधारक शिष्य,
गिरीश

व्यवस्थापक,

पुणे पुस्तक भंडार,
सदाशिव पेठ,
पुणे–३०

श्रीमान,

    कृपया खाली लिहिल्या प्रमाणे पुस्तके माझ्या पत्त्यावर पाठवावी, सोबत माझा पत्ता दिलेला आहे. पुस्तकांची यादी खालील प्रमाणे आहे.

१.   बाल भारती – पुस्तक चौथे – प्रति १

२.   अंक गणित बीज गणित – पुस्तक चौथे – प्रति १

३.   भारताचा इतिहास – भाग चौथा – प्रति १

वरील लिहीलेली पुस्तके वी०पी०पी० द्वारा पाठवावी. मी तुमचा आभारी आहे.

भवदीय
धनंजय

CHAPTER 8
PROVERBS
(म्हणी)

A

A figure among ciphers.
वासरात लंगडी गाय शहाणी.

A drop in the ocean.
दर्यामें खसखस.

An ass went to ask for horns but lost his ears.
करायला गेलो एक पण झाले दुसरेच.

As long as there is life, there is hope.
श्वास आहे तोपर्यंत आशा आहे.

As you sow so shall you reap.
करावे तसे भरावे.

B

Barking dogs seldom bite
जे (ढग) गर्जतात ते पडत नाहीत.

(A) bad workman quarrels with his tools.
नाचता येईना आंगण वाकडे.

(A) bad man is better than a bad name.
वाईट माणूस बरा पण कलंक वाईट.

Better wear your shoes than your bad clothes
बेकारीपेक्षा बिगारी बरी.

Birds of the same feather.
एका माळेचे मणी.

C

(to) Carry coal to new castle.
प्रयागलाच गंगा नेणे.

Cast in the same mould.
एकाच माळेचे मणी.

Curst cows have short horns.
कुत्र्याचे शेपूट बारा वर्ष नळीत घालून ठेवले तरी वाकडे ते वाकडेच.

Cut your coat according to cloth.
अंथरूण पाहून पाय पसरावे.

(a) Contented mind is a contented feast.
संतोष परम्सुखम्.

Coming events cast their shadows before.
मुलाचे पाय पाळण्यात दिसतात.

Charity must begin at home.
स्बत:पासून दानधर्म.

D

Dry bread at home is better than sweatmeat abroad.
घरची शिळी भाकरी चांगली बाहेरची मिठाई नको.

Distant drums sound well.
दुरून डोंगर साजरे.

Do good and forget it.
निष्काम कर्म करा.

(the) desperate man does all things.
मरायला तयार झालेला मनुष्य वाटेल ते करायला भीत नाही.

E

Every cock fights best on this own dunghill.
आपल्या गल्लीत कुत्रासुद्धा वाघ बनतो.

Every potter praises his own pot.
आपला तो बाब्या.

Earth's joys and heaven's combined.
दुधात साखर पडणे.

Empty vessels make much noise.
उथळ पाण्याला खळखळाट फार.

Every dog has its day.
चार दिवस सासूचे चार दिवस सुनेचे.

F

Friendship with a mean fellow is always dreadful.
असंगाशी संग, प्राणाशी गाठ.

First come first served:
पहिला आला तो भला.

Fortune favours the brave.
साहसे श्री : प्रतिवसती.

G

Good mind good find.
आपण चांगले तर जग चांगले.

(a) Good servant should have good wages.
दाम तसे काम.

(a) Good word costs nothing.
गुळ देऊ नका, गोड तर बोला.

(a) Good name is better than bags of gold.
इभ्रतीसाठी लाखाची हानी झाली तरी चिंता करु नये.

God helps those who help themselves.
धैर्याने काम करणाऱ्याला परमेश्वर मदत करतो.

H

Haste makes waste.
घाईने काम खराब होते.

He who grasps all things will lose all.
हातचे सोडून पळत्याच्या पाठी लागणे.

Handsome is that handsome does.
सद्गुणीच सुस्वरुप.

He gives thrice who gives in a trice.
वेळेवर केलेली मदत फार लाभदायक होते.

Hedges have eyes and walls have ears.
भिंतीला सुद्धा कान असतात.

How long will the mother's prayers avail to save her kid.

बकऱ्याची आई त्याला कुठवर उपणार.

I

It takes two to make a quarrel.

एका हाताने टाळी वाजत नाही.

It is a silly fish that is caught with the same bait.

एकदा फसला म्हणून पुन्हा पुन्हा फरास नाही.

It is a hard winter when dogs eat dogs.

डाकीणसुद्धा आपले मूल खात नाही.

If the sky falls we shall gather larks.

काम करायचें नसेल तेव्हा विलक्षण अटी घालतात.

It is money that buys the land.

दाम करी काम.

Ill-got, ill-spent.

माल फुकटात मिळाला म्हणजे वाटेल तसा वापरला जातो.

It is dark under the lamp.

दिव्याखाली अंधार.

K

Knowlegde is more powerful than mere strength.

शक्तीपेक्ष युक्ती श्रेष्ठ.

(to) Kill two birds with one stone.

एका दगडाने दोन पक्षी मारणे.

L

(a) Low-born person feels proud of his honour.
माकाडाच्या हाती काकडा.

Light reflects light.
सेवा कर नि मेवा खा.

Little knowledge is a dangerous thing.
अर्धवट वैद्य असला म्हणजे जीव धोक्यांत पडावयाचाच.

Let the past bury its dead, think of ahead.
झाले गेले गंगेला मिळाले, आती पुढचा विचार करा.

Like father like son.
बाप तसा बेटा.

M

(the) Master's eye makes the mare fat.
धनी स्वतः लक्ष देईल तरच शेती वाढेल.

Much ado about nothing.
डोंगर पोखरून उंदीर काढला.

Money, woman and land are the roots of all troubles.
सोने, जमीन आणि स्त्री हे भांडणाचे मूळ आहे.

Man proposes God disposes.
मनुष्य पळी जमवितो आणि देव बुधला सांडतो.

Money begets money.
पैशाकडे पैसा जातो.

(a) Nine days' wonder.

तेरड्याचा रंग तीन दिवस.

Near the church further from heaven.

दिव्याखाली अंधेर.

Neither fish or fowl.

इकडचे नाही आणि तिकडचे नाही.

New brooms are not better than old ones.

नव्याचे नऊ दिवस, जुन्याचे शंभर दिवस.

Necessity has no law.

गरजेला कायदा नाही.

No pains no gains.

श्रमाविना फायदा नाही.

O

One post and one hundred candidates.

वस्तु थोडी व मागणी फार.

One fish infects the whole water.

एक नासका आंबा आढीतील सर्व आंबे नासवतो.

P

Practice makes perfect.

जात्यावर बसले की ओवी सुचते.

(a) prophet is not honoured in his own country.
पिकते तेथे विकत नाही.

(the) priest goes no further from the church.
सरड्याची धाव कुंपणापर्यंत.

R

Respect yourself and you will be respected.
आपली पत आपल्याच हाती असते.

(a) robber in the garb of a saint.
रामनाम जपायचे व दुसऱ्याचा माल लुबाडायचा.

Rod is the logic of fools.
नीच मनुष्य लाथ खाल्लयाशिवाय सरळ मार्गावर येत नाही.

Rome was not built in a day.
तूप खाल्ले की लगेच रुप नाही.

S

Self-praise is no recommendation.
आपणच आपली स्तुति करणे.

Small cost and great show.
थोड्या खर्चात उत्तम काम होणे.

(to) swallow a camel, to strain at gnat.
हत्ती जातो पण मुंगी जात नाही.

Service is no inheritance.
नोकरीला स्थिरता नसते.

174

Singing all the days in the week and going to church on Sundays.

करुन करुन भागली आणि देव पुजायला लागली.

Spend and God will send.

नशोबवानाला देव देती.

T

To talk much is not good.

फार बोलणे चांगले नाही.

To err is human.

चूक करणे हा मनुष्य स्वभाव आहे.

Throwing pearls before swine.

गाढवापुढे गीता वाचणे.

Two of a trade seldom agree.

एका म्यानात दोन तलवारी राहू शकत नाहीत.

Time and tide wait for none.

गेलेली संधी पुन्हा येत नाही.

Traitors are the worst enemies.

घरभेद्या माणूस राष्ट्राचा नाश करतो.

U

Union is strength.

एकता हेच बळ.

W

When I am dead, the world is gone.
आपण मेलो जग बुडाले.

When buffaloes fight crops suffer.
सुक्याबरोबर ओले जळते.

When you go to Rome, do as the Romans do.
देश तसा वेश.

Wisdom is the daughter of old age.
पिकल्या केसांना काही अनुभव असतो.

(a) wolf in lamb's skin.
तोंडाने मित्रत्वाच्या गोष्टी बोलून मनात वैर धरणे.

Y

Your bread is buttered on both sides.
लाभच लाभ होणे.

(the) younger is even worse than the elder.
मोठ्यापेक्षा छोटा आणखी वाईट.

Your schemes won't work here.
माझ्यापुढे तुमची लुच्चेगिरी चालणार नाही.

ओझे a load   कौतुक admiration

176

CHAPTER 9
VOCABULARY

अखेर finally
आबाद populated
आरसा mirror
आराम rest
आशा hope
आहार food
अजून yet
अटक arrest
अतिथि guest
आधाशी greedy
आंधळा blind
अंधार darkness
अंगरक्षक bodyguard
इच्छा wish
इतर other
इमानदार honest
इसम a person
इंजिन engine
व्यवस्था arrangement
इंग्रजी English

इंधन fuel
ईर्ष्या jealousy
उकरणे to dig
उखाणा a riddle
उघडा haked
उचकी hiccough
उजळ bright
उंच high, tall
उंचवटा a mound
उंची height
ऊन sunshine
उष्मा heat
ऊस sugarcane
ऊत ebullition
ऋषि saint
एकटा alone
येथे here
ऐट pomp
ऐसा such
ओटा the lap

ओझे a load
औषध medicine
कचरा dust

कडक brittle
कठीण difficult
कडी a chain
कदाचित् perhaps
कागद paper
कायदा law
कापूस cotton
कातरी scissors
काबू control
किंमत price
किल्ली key
किशोर youth
कीर्ति fame
कीव pity
कुंचा a brush
कुटी a hut
कुटुंब family
कुरळे curly
केन्द्रीय central
कैदी prisoner
कोपरा corner
कोमल soft
कोळसा charcoal

कौतुक admiration
क्रिया an act
क्रीडा playing,
   sporting
क्रूर cruel
क्रोध anger
खजिना treasure
खडा pebble
खडू chalk
खड्डा a pit
खबर news
खलनायक villain
खाडी an inlet
खाण a mine
खात्री guarantee
खिन्न depressed
खेळाडू a player
खीळ a bolt
खुंटी a peg
खुनी murderer
खुद्द personally
खुळा crazy
स्वेटर a footwear
खेडवळ boorish
खेप trip
खोड bad habit
खोडी a defect

गच्ची terrace
गजर alarm
गड hillfort
गद्य prose
गंध smell
गप्पा chitchatting
गबर rich
गुपचुप silent
गरजू needy
गर्व pride
गर्विष्ठ proud
गाडी a cart
गादी bed
गार cold
गुण merit
गुणी talented
गुप्त hidden
गुहा cave
गोल round
गोप्य secret
ग्रह a planet
घडण shape
घडी a fold, a period
घाट a pass
घाम sweat

घेणे to take
चटई mat
चतुर clever
चमक glitter
चरित्र character
चर्चा discussion
चलाख smart
चश्मा, चष्मा spectacles
चाक wheel
चाचरणे to falter
चामडे leather
चिंधी rag
चूक mistake
छळ harassment
जग world
जनता people
जुळा twin
जोखमी risky
झगडा clash
झगा frock
झाडणे to sweep
झोका a swing
टणक hard
टवटवीत fresh
टिकवणे to keep up

टोला stroke	दटाविणे intimidate
ठक thief	दडपण pressure
ठसा stamp	दर्जा status
ठिणगी spark	दान gift
डाकू dacoit	दिशा direction
डाग sopt	दुर्गुण vice
पर्वत, डोंगर mountain	दृष्टि vision
ढकलणे to push	देश country
ढाल shield	दोघे both
ढास trycough	धका shock
तक्रार complaint	धीर patience
तडफ elan	धुरकट smoky
तंतु thread	ध्यान contemplation
तलवार sword	नक्कल copy
तस्वीर portrait	नर्तक dancer
ताईत talisman	घोषणा slogan
तळणे to fry	नाग cobra
तीर arrow	निकामी unserviceable
तुटणे break	निघणे to go out
थकवा exhaustion	नैसर्गिक nature
थडगे tomb	पंक्ति row
थाप bluff	पंख wing
थारा shelter	प्रगति progress
थोर great	पाणिग्रहण wedding
दगड stone	पिंजरा cage
दगा fraud	पोहणे to swim

प्रसिद्ध famous
फडताळ cupboard
फाळणी partition
फुंकणे to blow
फोल invain
बटवा purse
बहिरा deaf
बरणी jar
बाहुली doll
बुजरा shy
बुडणे drown
भक्त devotee
भागीदार partner
भिक्षा alms
भूक hunger
भूक hole
भोळा innocent
भिकारी beggar
मऊ soft
मोजा sock
मूर्ख foolish
मत्सर envy
मागणे to ask for
मुक्ति liberty
मोकळा free
मोडका broken

मोहक attractive
म्हातारा old person
यंत्र machine
युग era
यत्न effort
येथे here
यात्री pilgrim
योग्य perfect
रक्त, रुधिर blood
रान forest
रीळ reel
रडणे to weep
रेशीम silk
लबाड cunning
लांब distant
लोटी water-pot
लवकर immediately
वक्ता speaker
वाम left
वर up
वर्तमान current
वाणिज्य commerce
शस्त्र weapon
शब्द word
शुद्ध pure
सत्य truth

सुगंध fragrance

स्वार्थ selfishness

सैल loose

संमति permission

सहज casual

सागर, समुद्र sea

हक़ right

होकार affirmative answer

क्षमा pardon

CHAPTER 10
Abbreviations

A1–first class... प्रथम दर्जाचा

A.B.C.–the rudiments...मूलतत्त्वे

A.C.C.– Auxiliary Cadet Corps
....शाळांतील लष्करी शिक्षण घेणारी तुकडी

A.D.C.–aide-de-camp... शरीररक्षक

A.G.–Accountant-General... प्रमुख हिशेबनीस

Asst.–Assistant... मदतनीस

B.A.–Bachelor of Arts. ... कला स्नातक

B.Ag.–Bachelor of Agriculture... शेतकी स्नातक

B.Com.–Bachelor of Commerce... वाणिज्य स्नातक

B.D.–Bachelor of Divinity... धर्म स्नातक

C.A.–Chartered Accountant... सनदी हिशेबनीस

C.I.D.–Criminal Investigation Department गुन्हा
अन्वेषण विभाग

D.L.O.–Dead Letter Office... बेपत्ता पत्रांची कचेरी

E & O.E.–Errors and Omissions Excepted... भूलचूक
वगळून

183

F.M.–Field Marshal... अत्युच्च सेनापति

F.O.–Foreign Office... परराष्ट्र कचेरी

G.H.O.–General Headquarters... मुख्य छावणी

G.P.O.–General Post Office... प्रमुख टपाल कचेरी

H.G.–Home Guard... गृहरक्षक

I.A.S.–Indian Administrative Service... भारतीय सनदी सेवा

I.D.–Intelligence Department... गुप्त हेरखाते

I.O.U.–I owe you... कर्जाचे वचनपत्र

M.L.A.–Member Legislative Assembly... विधानसभा सदस्य

M.L.C.–Member Legislative Council... विधानपरिषद सदस्य

O.K.–All Correct... ठाकठीक

T.A.–Travelling Allowance... प्रवास भत्ता

V.I.P.–Very Important Person... अति विशिष्ट व्यक्ती